# THE HEART OF DŌGEN'S

# *Shōbōgenzō*

*translated and annotated by*

NORMAN WADDELL AND MASAO ABE

STATE UNIVERSITY OF NEW YORK PRESS

Published by
STATE UNIVERSITY OF NEW YORK PRESS, ALBANY

© 2002 State University of New York

All rights reserved

Printed in the United States of America

For information, contact State University of New York Press, Albany, NY
www.sunypress.edu

Production, Laurie Searl
Marketing, Fran Keneston

**Library of Congress Cataloging-in-Publication Data**

Dogen, 1200–1253
  [Shōbōgenzō. English]
  The heart of Dogen's Shōbōgenzō / translated and annotated by Norman Waddell and Masao Abe.
    p.  cm.
  Includes bibliographical references and index.
  ISBN 0–7914–5241–7 (hc. : alk. paper) — ISBN 0–7914–5242–8 (pbk. : alk. paper)
    1. Sōtōshū—Doctrines—Early works to 1800. I. Waddell, Norman, 1940– .
  II. Abe, Masao, 1915– . III. Title.

BQ9499.D654 S5613  2002
294.3'85—dc21

                                                        2001044661

10 9 8 7 6 5 4 3 2 1

# CONTENTS

# ABBREVIATIONS

CTL:    *Ching-te ch'uan-teng lu* 景德伝灯録. T51. 2076

LTHY:   *Lien-teng hui-yao* 聯灯会要. ZZ2b.9.3-5

Ōkubo:  *Dōgen Zenji zenshū* 道元禅師全集, 2 vols., Tokyo, 1969

SBGZ:  *Shōbōgenzō* 正法眼蔵: Ōkubo, vol. 1.

T:      *Taishō shinshū daizōkyō* 大正新修大蔵経. Tokyo, 1914–1922.

ZZ:    *Dai-Nihon zoku-zōkyō* 大日本続蔵経, Kyoto, 1905–1912.

# TRANSLATORS' INTRODUCTION

This book offers annotated translations of eight key fascicles from *Shōbōgenzō*, the major work of Dōgen Kigen, 1200–1253, founder of Japanese Sōtō Zen. Among the fascicles translated are four—*Bendōwa*, *Genjōkōan*, *Busshō*, and *Uji*—that the Sōtō school has regarded as representing the heart of the entire collection. We have also included a translation of *Fukanzazengi*, a brief but important text on the principles of zazen (seated Zen meditation).

Aside from a few autobiographical references found in Dōgen's own writings, the particulars of his life are known largely through the early biographical records compiled many years after his death by priests in his Sōtō lineage.[1] According to these traditional accounts, Dōgen was of noble birth, his father an important figure at the imperial court, and his mother a daughter of the powerful Fujiwara clan.

He began his monastic study at age thirteen at Yokawa, the center of Tendai esotericism on Mount Hiei near Kyoto. He later spent time at the nearby Onjō-ji (Miidera), a rival Tendai monastery situated in the foothills of Mount Hiei. He then moved to the Kennin-ji, a Tendai temple in Kyoto where in preceding decades the Tendai priest Myōan Eisai (1141–1215) had been introducing the teachings and practice methods of Chinese Zen, which he had acquired from teachers of the then dominant Lin-chi (in Japanese, Rinzai) lineage during two trips to China.

---

1. Although probably fairly reliable in their broader outlines, there is a natural tendency toward hagiography in these records. Only recently have scholars begun to reexamine the traditional accounts of Dōgen's life, and details heretofore accepted as fact are now being called into question. Eventually this reassessment should result in a clearer overall picture of his career, especially in such areas as his early monastic life and the circumstances surrounding the teaching he engaged in immediately after his return from China. As our main concern in the present book is to present the religious thought of *Shōbōgenzō*, we have made no attempt to address these or other current trends in Dōgen studies. The most recent works in Japanese that deal comprehensively with Dōgen's life are by Nakaseko Shōdō, *Dōgen Zenji den kenkyū* (Tokyo, 1979) and *Dōgen Zenji den kenkyū, zoku* (Tokyo, 1997).

Dōgen entered Kennin-ji around 1217, and for seven years he studied under Eisai's student Myōzen (1184–1225). In 1223, he accompanied Myōzen to China, where he visited Lin-chi masters at leading monasteries, including the Ching-te ssu on Mount T'ien-t'ung. In June 1225, at the Ching-te ssu, Dōgen encountered Ts'ao-tung (Japanese, Sōtō) teacher Ju-ching (1163–1228). He studied under Ju-ching for a little over two years, during which time he achieved enlightenment and received Ju-ching's Dharma transmission.

Dōgen returned to Japan in 1227, at age twenty-eight, and he took up residence once again at the Kennin-ji in Kyoto. He was now a certified teacher in the Ts'ao-tung Zen lineage, the teachings of which were still unknown in Japan. The remaining twenty-five years of his life, the first fifteen of which were spent in the Kyoto area, the remaining ten in the remote mountains of Echizen province (modern Fukui prefecture), were devoted to teaching and writing, setting down in Shōbōgenzō and various other works the essentials of his teaching and the rules and standards for monastic life that he wished to establish in Japan.

The first of these works, Fukanzazengi, a brief composition in Chinese, sets forth the basic principles of zazen as the authentic method of Buddhist practice. It was composed the year he returned from China, while he was residing at Kennin-ji. He left Kennin-ji in 1230 for the An'yō-in, a small temple in Fukakusa, 6 or 7 kilometers south of Kyoto. A year later, in 1231, he wrote Bendōwa, a treatise in Japanese in which he once again promotes, this time at considerable length, the superior merits of zazen over all other forms of Buddhist practice, explaining in detail the various reasons for its primacy. Written when Dōgen was thirty-one, this early work already contains most of the essential themes he would later develop in the major fascicles of Shōbōgenzō. For this reason, Bendōwa has been long regarded as the best introduction to the collection as a whole.

In 1233, Dōgen moved from the An'yō-in to the nearby Kannondōri Kōshō-hōrin-ji (the name was later abbreviated to Kōshō-ji) and resided there for the next ten years, a decade that from a literary standpoint was the most important and productive of his life. During this period he wrote over forty fascicles of Shōbōgenzō. Among them were Genjōkōan, Ikka Myōju, Uji, and Busshō.

In 1243, Dōgen turned the abbotship of the Kōshō-ji over to one of his followers and left the Kyoto area for the remote province of Echizen. There, the following year, he founded the Daibutsu-ji (later renamed Eihei-ji), where he continued to teach and write for the final nine years of his life. He died in 1253 while on a trip to Kyoto seeking medical care for a chronic pulmonary illness thought to have been tuberculosis.

## SHŌBŌGENZŌ

*Shōbōgenzō* is a voluminous work, comprising well over half of the total wordage of all of Dōgen's remarkable literary output. It is in effect a collection of religious discourses, each one complete in itself, and each one devoted to a particular subject or theme relating to Zen teaching and practice. They were delivered or written between 1231, when he was thirty-one, and 1253, the year of his death. He seems to have planned an even 100 of these fascicles, but apparently he managed to complete final versions of only twelve. Dōgen's holographs of these texts, and the manuscripts of *Shōbōgenzō* transcribed by his followers, were copied and recopied by later generations of Sōtō priests. This has resulted in various different manuscript compilations of *Shōbōgenzō*, in sixty fascicles, seventy-five fascicles, twenty-eight fascicles, twelve fascicles, and so on, and it has also created knotty bibliographical problems that modern-day editors are still trying to sort out. Modern editions generally consist of ninety-five fascicles, and include all those Dōgen is thought to have intended for *Shōbōgenzō*, as well as a few—among them *Bendōwa* and *Shōji*—that were not originally composed for the collection but were inserted by later editors.

According to the explanation in the *Shōbōgenzō shō*, the earliest commentary on *Shōbōgenzō* compiled by Dōgen's student Kyōgō, Dōgen's title—which may be rendered "Treasury of the True Dharma Eye" (*Shō* 正: right, true—*bō* 法: Dharma—*gen* 眼: eye—*zō* 蔵: treasury)—is a reference to the Dharma itself, the fundamental principle of the Buddhist teaching. In a collection of Dōgen's sayings, compiled by his disciple Senne (n.d.), we are told that Dōgen had intended to call the collection *Shōbōgenzō nehan-myōshin* (Treasury of the True Dharma eye, Marvelous Mind of Nirvana)—a title derived from the words which Shakyamuni Buddha was said to have uttered in the first "mind-to-mind" transmission of the Zen Dharma[2]—but he finally settled for the shorter, truncated form *Shōbōgenzō*. The words *Shōbōgenzō* also reflect a distinction the Zen tradition likes to draw between itself and other Buddhist schools: whereas they base their doctrines on various sutras preached by the Buddha, Zen, as the "school of the Buddha-mind," transmits the very source of those sutras—the enlightened mind itself.

A large portion of the discourse in *Shōbōgenzō* consists of Dōgen's commentary on koans, stories, dialogues, and sayings in Chinese that he selected

---

2. According to Zen tradition, this transmission took place at Vulture Peak, when the Buddha, instead of delivering a sermon to the audience, held up a golden lotus flower. Among those present, only Mahakashyapa grasped his meaning, expressing his understanding with a smile. The Buddha thereupon confirmed Mahakashyapa's understanding with the words—"I have the True Dharma Eye, the Marvelous Mind of Nirvana. This I entrust to you, Mahakashyapa."

to elucidate aspects of his Zen teaching.[3] Similar koan collections with the comments of Chinese Zen teachers attached to them had been published in the century or so before Dōgen's birth, the most prominent examples of the genre being the *Ts'ung-jung lu, Pi-yen lu,* and *Cheng-fa yen-tsan.* The *Cheng-fa yen-tsan,* compiled in the middle of the twelfth century by Rinzai priest Ta-hui Tsung-kao (1089–1163), even bore the same title as Dōgen's work (*Shōbōgenzō* is the Japanese reading of *Cheng-fa yen-tsan*). It seems safe to assume that Dōgen was familiar with these previous collections and that they were the initial impetus for writing *Shōbōgenzō.* Even when that is said, however, *Shōbōgenzō* remains unique, even within the enormous literature of the Zen tradition. Nowhere else can we find another work in which a teacher undertakes such a lengthy and deliberately systematic and rational exposition of his religious thought and experience.

Until it was first published in 1811, *Shōbōgenzō* had existed only in manuscript form and was presumably little known outside of a small circle within the Sōtō hierarchy.[4] It was not until well into the twentieth century that it began to attract attention outside of the Buddhist priesthood. Since then, many leading philosophers, literary critics, and cultural historians, attracted to work for its philosophic content and literary merit, have attested to the importance and striking originality of Dōgen's thought.[5]

Over the past thirty years, *Shōbōgenzō* has become known beyond the confines of Japan, and even through the undeniably cloudy lens of translation it has now secured a place among the masterworks of the world's religious literature. Dōgen has become a regular subject of academic debate, and a number of comparative studies of Dōgen and Western thinkers such as Heidegger and Sartre have appeared. Particular attention has been given to the ontological bases of his thought, such as his realization that "all beings are the Buddhanature," and his emphasis on the identity of being and time.

TRANSLATION

It would be impractical to list all of the commentaries, old and new, that have been consulted in translating the texts and drafting the footnotes, but of the

---

3. Dōgen had, around 1235, compiled a collection of 300 koans in their original Chinese form titled *Shōbōgenzō sambyaku soku* 正法眼藏三百則 (*Ōkubo* vol. 2, 201–52). Dōgen cites or comments on roughly 100 of these 300 koans in *Shōbōgenzō.*

4. While it is generally true that access to *Shōbōgenzō* was limited by authorities in the Sōtō school, manuscript copies must have been available, since even prior to its initial appearance in print, quotations from *Shōbōgenzō* appear in the writings of Rinzai priests such as Mujaku Dōchū (1653–1744) and Hakuin Ekaku (1686–1768).

5. In his *Shōbōgenzō no tetsugaku shikan,* 1939, the philosopher Tanabe Hajime was the first to draw attention to the essentially philosophical nature of *Shōbōgenzō.*

earlier, religiously-oriented commentaries, Nishiari Bokuzan's *Shōbōgenzō keiteki* was a very helpful companion. The ten-volume variorum edition of *Shōbōgenzō*, *Shōbōgenzō chūkai zensho*, comprising all of the important pre-Meiji commentaries, contains mines of information that we have freely quarried. We also wish to acknowledge a deep debt to the late Nishitani Keiji, who was always there with encouragement and generous counsel to help us unravel the complexities of a text that is often extremely difficult to understand.

We began translating *Shōbōgenzō* in 1970. The first fascicle, *Bendōwa*, was published in the spring of 1971 in the *Eastern Buddhist*, a Buddhist journal published in Kyoto. Subsequent fascicles appeared serially over the next five or six years. All were translated jointly, except for *SBGZ Uji* [Being-Time], which was done by Waddell. Both translations and footnotes have been revised at intervals in the years since.

The translations are based on the text in *Dōgen Zenji zenshū*, a two-volume edition of Dōgen's complete writings compiled by Sōtō scholar Ōkubo Dōshū and published in 1971.

# ONE

# *Fukanzazengi*
# 普勧坐禅儀

## (UNIVERSAL PROMOTION OF
## THE PRINCIPLES OF ZAZEN)

*Fukanzazengi* is Dōgen's first work. It was written in 1227, the year he returned from China. It is influenced by and in many ways resembles a number of similar tracts on zazen that existed in China, such as the one by tenth-century priest Chang-lu Tsung-tse. All are composed in a highly rhetorical, easily memorized style of Chinese prose.

Dōgen declares that he considered his master Ju-ching "the only person since the T'ang master Po-chang who truly understood the significance of zazen." He praises Ju-ching for teaching that "sitting (zazen) is the Buddha Dharma and the Buddha Dharma is sitting." *Fukanzazengi* is Dōgen's first attempt to transmit this teaching to his countrymen.

*Fukanzazengi* has been recited at the regular night sitting and on other occasions in Sōtō Zen temples down through the centuries. Although it is not a part of the *Shōbōgenzō* collection, we have included it in the present book because of the important place it occupies in Dōgen's Zen.

In *Fukanzazengi senjutsu yurai* [Reason for Composing *Fukanzazengi*], Dōgen explains why he wrote the work:

> Since in Japan it has never been possible to learn about the "special trans-
> mission outside the scriptures" or the "treasure of the right Dharma eye,"

much less the principles of zazen, they are not transmitted here. So as soon as I returned home from the land of the Sung [China], and students began coming to me for instruction, I was obliged for their sakes to compile this work [Fukanzazengi] on the principles of zazen. Long ago, the Chinese Zen master Po-chang constructed a monastery with a hall set aside especially for zazen practice. In so doing he effectively transmitted the true style of the First Zen patriarch Bodhidharma. This style was distinct from the briars and brambles of word-attachment [of the Buddhist schools] that had preceded him. This is something that students should know and not be confused about.

There is a Tso-ch'an i (Japanese, Zazengi) by the priest Chang-lu Tsung–tse included in the Ch'an-yüan ch'ing-kuei [Pure Regulations for the Zen Gardens]. For the most part it follows Po-chang's original intent, but it also contains some additions made by Tsung-tse himself. This has resulted in errors of various kinds, as well as an overall lack of clarity. No one who does not already know the meaning behind the words can fully understand what he is trying to say. For that reason, I have now gathered together and written down the true principles of zazen that I learned [in Sung China] in hopes that they will transmit the inexpressible heart of the Buddha-patriarchs. (Ōkubo, vol. 2, 3–4)

A comparison of the Fukanzazengi with the Tso-ch'an i by Tsung-tse shows that while Dōgen often merely appropriated the text of the earlier work, he also changed and added portions to rectify what he regarded as mistakes or ambiguities in Tsung-tse's work.

## FUKANZAZENGI

The Way is originally perfect and all-pervading. How could it be contingent upon practice and realization? The Dharma-vehicle is utterly free and untrammeled. What need is there for our concentrated effort? Indeed, the Whole Body is far beyond the world's dust. Who could believe in a means to brush it clean?[1] It is never apart from you right where you are. What use is there going off here and there to practice?

---

1. The Whole Body [of reality] (tathatā) refers to the totality of things in their suchness; the Buddha-nature. The world's "dust," giving rise to illusions, defiles the original purity of the Buddha-nature.

A means to brush it clean is an allusion to the famous verse contest by which the Sixth Zen Patriarch Hui-neng received the Dharma transmission from the Fifth Patriarch Hung-jen. The verse of Shen-hsiu, Hung-jen's chief disciple, was: "This body is the Bodhi tree; the mind like a bright mirror on a stand. Constantly strive to brush it clean. Do not allow dust to collect." Hui-neng responded with the verse: "Basically, Bodhi is not a tree. Neither does the mind-mirror have a stand. From the first there is not a single thing, so where can dust collect?" (CTL, ch. 5).

And yet if there is the slightest discrepancy, the Way is as distant as heaven from earth. If the least like or dislike arises, the mind is lost in confusion.[2] Suppose you gain pride of understanding, inflate your own achievement, glimpse the wisdom that runs through all things, attain the Way and clarify your mind, raising an aspiration to escalade the very sky. You are making an initial, partial excursion through the frontiers of the Dharma,[3] but you are still deficient in the vital Way of total emancipation.

Look at the Buddha himself, who was possessed of great inborn knowledge—the influence of his six years of upright sitting is noticeable still. Or Bodhidharma, who transmitted the Buddha's mind-seal—the fame of his nine years of wall sitting is celebrated to this day. Since this was the case with the saints of old, how can people today dispense with negotiation of the Way?

You should therefore cease from practice based on intellectual understanding, pursuing words and following after speech, and learn the backward step that turns your light inward to illuminate your self. Body and mind will drop away of themselves, and your original face will manifest itself. If you wish to attain suchness, you should practice suchness without delay.

For the practice of Zen, a quiet room is suitable. Eat and drink moderately. Cast aside all involvements, and cease all affairs. Do not think good, do not think bad. Do not administer pros and cons. Cease all the movements of the conscious mind, the gauging of all thoughts and views. Have no designs on becoming a Buddha. The practice of Zen (*sanzen*) has nothing whatever to do with the four bodily attitudes of moving, standing, sitting, or lying down.

At the place where you regularly sit, spread out a layer of thick matting and place a cushion on it. Sit either in the full-lotus or half-lotus posture. In the full-lotus posture, you first place your right foot on your left thigh and your left foot on your right thigh. In the half-lotus, you simply press your left foot against your right thigh. You should have your robes and belt loosely bound and arranged in order. Then place your right hand on your left leg and your left palm facing upwards on your right palm, thumb-tips touching. Sit upright in correct bodily posture, inclining neither to the left nor the right, leaning neither forward nor backward. Be sure your ears are on a plane with your shoulders and your nose in line with your navel. Place your tongue against the front roof

---

2. From the Zen verse *Hsinhsinming*: "If there is the slightest discrepancy, the Way is as distant as heaven from earth. To realize its manifestation, be neither for nor against. The conflict of likes and dislikes is in itself the disease of the mind. . . . Do not dwell in dualities, and scrupulously avoid pursuing the Way. If there is the least like or dislike, the mind is lost in confusion."

3. Dharma (*hō* 法): Truth, Law, the doctrine and teaching of the Buddha, Buddhism. Throughout this translation, "Dharma" refers to Truth, and "dharma(s)" refers to things, the elements of existence, phenomena.

of your mouth, with teeth and lips both shut. Your eyes should always remain open. You should breathe gently through your nose.

Once you have adjusted yourself into this posture, take a deep breath, inhale, exhale, rock your body to the right and left, and settle into a steady, unmoving sitting position. Think of not-thinking. How do you think of not-thinking? Nonthinking.[4] This in itself is the essential art of zazen.

The zazen I speak of is not learning meditation. It is simply the Dharma-gate of repose and bliss. It is the practice-realization of totally culminated enlightenment. It is things as they are in suchness. No traps or snares can ever reach it. Once its heart is grasped, you are like the dragon when he reaches the water, like the tiger when he enters the mountain. You must know that when you are doing zazen, right there the authentic Dharma is manifesting itself, striking aside dullness and distraction from the first.

When you arise from sitting, move slowly and quietly, calmly and deliberately. Do not rise suddenly or abruptly. In surveying the past, we find that transcendence of ignorance and enlightenment, and dying while sitting or standing, have all depended entirely on the strength gained through zazen.[5]

Moreover, enlightenment brought on by the opportunity provided by a finger, a banner, a needle, or a mallet, the realization effected by the aid of a fly whisk, a fist, a staff, or a shout, cannot be fully comprehended by human discrimination.[6] It cannot be fully known by the practice-realization of super-natural powers.[7] It is activity beyond human hearing and seeing, a principle prior to human knowledge or perception.

---

4. These words appear in a dialogue that Dōgen makes the subject of SBGZ Zazenshin: A monk asked Yüeh-shan, "What does one think of when sitting motionlessly in zazen?" Yüeh-shan replied, "You think of not-thinking." "How do you think of not-thinking?" asked the monk. "Nonthinking," answered Yüeh-shan.

5. According to the Zen histories, Bodhidharma and the Fourth, Fifth, and Sixth Chinese patriarchs died while seated in zazen. The Third Patriarch died standing under a large tree.

6. These are allusions to the means that Zen masters use to bring students to enlightenment. Chü-chih's "One-finger Zen" is the subject of Case 3 of the Wu-men-kuan. When Ananda asked Kashyapa if the Buddha had transmitted anything to him besides the golden surplice, Kashyapa called out to him. When Ananda responded, Kashyapa told him to take down the banner at the gate, whereupon Ananda attained enlightenment. The Fifteenth Indian Zen Patriarch, Kanadeva, paid a visit to Nagarjuna. Nagarjuna, without saying a word, instructed an attendant to place a bowl brimming with water before his guest. Kanadeva took up a needle and dropped it into the bowl. As a result of this act, Nagarjuna accepted him as his disciple. One day when Shakyamuni ascended to the teaching-seat, the Bodhisattva Monju (Manjushri) rapped his gavel to signify the opening of the sermon, declaring, "Clearly understood is the Dharma, the royal Dharma. The Dharma, the royal Dharma, is thus," words usually uttered at the close of a sermon. Shakyamuni, without saying a word, left the teaching seat and retired.

7. The supernatural powers (jinzū 神通) are possessed by beings of exceptional spiritual attainment, enabling them unrestricted freedom of activity, eyes capable of seeing everywhere, ears of hearing all sounds, and so on. Dōgen says that the means used by a master in bringing

This being the case, intelligence, or lack of it, does not matter. No distinction exists between the dull and sharp-witted. If you concentrate your effort single-mindedly, you are thereby negotiating the Way with your practice-realization undefiled.[8] As you proceed along the Way, you will attain a state of everydayness.[9]

The Buddha-mind seal, whose customs and traditions extend to all things, is found in both India and China, both in our own world and in other worlds as well. It is simply a matter of devotion to sitting, total commitment to immovable sitting. Although it is said that there are as many minds as there are people, all of them must negotiate the Way solely in zazen. Why leave behind your proper place, which exists right in your own home, and wander aimlessly off to the dusty realms of other lands?[10] If you make even a single misstep, you stray from the Great Way lying directly before you.

You have gained the pivotal opportunity of human form. Do not let your time pass in vain. You are maintaining the essential function of the Buddha Way. Would you take meaningless delight in the spark from a flintstone?[11] Form and substance are like dewdrops on the grass, destiny like the dart of lightning—vanishing in an instant, disappearing in a flash.

Honored followers of Zen—you who have been long accustomed to groping for the elephant—please do not be suspicious of the true dragon.[12] Devote

---

students to enlightenment are not only beyond human thought, they are also beyond such supernormal powers. Moreover, there is nothing mysterious or supernatural about it; it is normal, everyday activity.

8. Since negotiating the Way (practice-realization) in zazen is practice-realization of ultimate reality, it is beyond all the defiling distinctions and dualities arising from conscious striving.

9. This is an allusion to a dialogue between Chao-chou and his master Nan-ch'üan. Chao-chou asked, "What is the Way?" Nan-ch'üan said, "Your everyday mind, that is the Way." "Well, does one proceed along it, or not?" asked Chao-chou. "Once you think about going forward, you go wrong," replied Nan-ch'üan (CTL, ch. 8).

10. An allusion to the parable of the lost son from the Lotus Sutra. An only son left his home and family to live in a distant land. He experienced great hardship, totally unaware of the increasing wealth his father was accumulating in the meantime. Many years later, the son returned home and inherited the great treasure that was his original birthright.

11. Spark from a flintstone is a metaphor often used to describe the brevity of human life.

12. An allusion to the well-known story from the Nirvana Sutra of a king who brought an elephant before a group of blind men and had them touch different parts of it. When he asked each of them to describe the beast, they gave widely diverse answers due to the limited nature of their individual experiences.

The true dragon is an allusion to a story in the Latter Han History about a man named Yeh Kung-tzu who had a passion for dragons. He had paintings and carvings of dragons throughout his house. One day a real dragon, hearing about Yeh's obsession, descended from the sky to pay him a visit. It poked its head through Yeh's front window, scaring him witless. Dōgen is insinuating that the Japanese of his time, ignorant of the true Dharma, had acquired a passion for false teachings. He tells them that now that he has brought them the real Dharma, they should not doubt its truth.

your energy to a Way that points directly to suchness. Revere the person of complete attainment beyond all human agency.[13] Gain accord with the enlightenment of the Buddhas. Succeed to the legitimate lineage of the patriarchs' samadhi. Constantly comport yourselves in such a manner and you are assured of being a person such as they. Your treasure-store will open of itself, and you will use it at will.

---

13. Since zazen is the practice of total reality, everyone who engages in it is a "person of complete attainment beyond all human agency" (*zetsugaku mui nin* 絶学無為人), a descriptive phrase from the *Cheng-tao ko*.

# TWO

# Bendōwa

# 辨道話

## (Negotiating the Way)

*Bendōwa*, the second work Dōgen wrote after his return from China, is a treatise on zazen practice as the "right entrance" to the Dharma. A colophon states that it was "written mid-autumn [the fifteen day of the eighth month], the third year of Kangi [1231], by Shamon Dōgen, a Dharma-transmitter who has travelled to China." *Bendōwa* seems to have been forgotten, and almost unknown, until it was rediscovered in manuscript in the Edo period. *Bendōwa* was not originally intended for *Shōbōgenzō*; it does not appear in any of the early redactions of the work. It was first included in *Shōbōgenzō* in a manuscript version dated 1684. It was first published, in a single-volume edition, in 1788. *Bendōwa* is often said to contain within it the essence of all ninety-five fascicles of *Shōbōgenzō*. It thus serves as an excellent introduction to the work. No doubt because of that, modern editions include it as the first fascicle in the collection.

   *Bendōwa* is divided into two sections. In the first, roughly one-fourth of the whole, Dōgen upholds the supremacy of zazen practice vis-à-vis all other Buddhist practices. He gives a concise exposition of the *jijuyū* samadhi, tells of his pilgrimage in search of the Dharma in Japan and China, and traces the transmission of this samadhi from Shakyamuni Buddha through the Chinese Zen masters of the T'ang and Sung dynasties.

   The remaining three-quarters of the work is arranged as a series of questions and answers, a popular format in religious treatises of this nature. Dōgen uses this format to give and defend his reasons for advocating the merits of zazen, and at the same time he tries to counter such questions and doubts as might arise in the minds of Buddhist acolytes and adherents of other Buddhist schools (Ōkubo, vol. 1, pp. 729–46).

## BENDŌWA

Buddha-tathagatas all have a wonderful means, unexcelled and free from human agency, for transmitting the wondrous Dharma and realizing supreme and complete awakening. That this means is only passed directly from Buddha to Buddha without deviation is due to the *jijuyū* samadhi, which is its touch-stone.[1]

To disport oneself freely in this samadhi, the right entrance is proper sitting in zazen. The Dharma is amply present in every person, but without practice, it is not manifested; without realization, it is not attained. It is not a question of one or many; let loose of it and it fills your hands. It is not bounded vertically or horizontally; speak it and it fills your mouth. Within this Dharma, Buddhas dwell everlastingly, leaving no perceptions in any sphere or direction; all living beings use it unceasingly, with no sphere or direction appearing in their perceptions.[2]

The negotiation of the Way with concentrated effort that I now teach

---

1. For Dōgen, who often employs duplicatives, or near-duplicatives, for emphasis, the terms *Buddha* and *Tathagata* ("one who has come from suchness," an epithet used to describe a Buddha) are virtually interchangeable.

*Free from human agency* translates the term *mui* 無為.

*Transmitting the wondrous Dharma* (*tanden* 单伝): The Dharma is said to be passed from Buddha to Buddha as water is transferred from one bowl to another. For Dōgen, this is *yuibutsu yobutsu* 唯佛与佛 ("only Buddha and Buddha"). Transmission of the Dharma can occur only between one Buddha and another.

Throughout *SBGZ*, the word *realize* (*shō* 証) implies realizing (making real), proving, confirming the Dharma in oneself.

*Supreme and complete awakening* translates *anoku bodai* 阿耨菩提, an abbreviated Chinese rendering of the Sanskrit *anuttara-samyak-sambodhi*, supreme and perfect enlightenment.

*Jijuyū samadhi* (*jijuyū sammai* 自受用三昧) signifies a state of samadhi in which an awakened one "receives" (*ju*) and "employs" (*yū*) the joy of awakening "in himself" (*ji*). (Shakyamuni, following his attainment, is said to have been self-immersed in the joy of enlightenment.) This personal enjoyment (*jijuyū*) is sometimes distinguished from *tajuyū* 他受用, which refers to the activity of aiding others (*ta*) to attain awakening so that they too can experience the joy of awakening. Here Dōgen uses the term *jijuyū* samadhi in an absolute sense, without distinguishing between it and *tajuyū*, with *jijuyū* being the basic source of *tajuyū* and including *tajuyū* in its own development. For Dōgen, the *jijuyū* samadhi is zazen, because zazen is a fundamental practice that includes both self-awakening and the awakening of all beings in the universe.

2. This describes the two aspects of *jijuyū* samadhi that are essentially inseparable: the aspect of Buddhas who dwell in this samadhi, having no attachment to any sphere of the objective world, and the aspect of all living beings who function in the same samadhi, whose perceptions are not limited by any sphere of the objective world. Here *perceptions* are not only those of the five senses but include those of the conscious mind as well.

makes myriad dharmas exist in realization and, in transcending realization, practices a total reality.[3] Then, when you are over the barrier, with all bonds cast off, you are no longer affected by such segmented distinctions.

After the religious mind arose in me, awakening the desire to seek the Way, I visited many religious teachers throughout the country. I chanced to encounter the priest Myōzen of Kennin-ji.[4] Swiftly passed the frosts and flowers of the nine years I studied with him. During that time I learned something of the manner of the Rinzai school. As the chief disciple of the patriarch Eisai, it was Myōzen alone who genuinely transmitted the supreme Buddha Dharma.[5] None of Eisai's other followers could compare with him.

After that, I proceeded to great Sung China, where I visited leading priests of the Liang-che region[6] and learned of the characteristics of the Five Zen Gates. Finally, I practiced under Zen master Ju-ching[7] at Mount T'ai-pai,[8] and there I resolved the one great matter of Zen practice for my entire life.[9] Then, when I returned home, in the first year of the She-ting period of the Sung [1228],[10] my thoughts immediately turned to preaching the Dharma for the salvation of my fellow beings—it was as though I had taken a heavy burden upon my shoulders. Nevertheless, in order to await the time when I can work vigorously to this end and unburden myself of the desire to spread the Dharma far and wide, I am for the time being living like a cloud or water plant, drifting

---

3. *Transcending realization: shutsuro* 出路: As long as one remains within realization after transcending the realm of differentiation, complete liberation is unachieved. Complete liberation requires transcending realization as well and reentering the realm of differentiation in order to work for the salvation of others. "Total reality" 一如 (*ichinyo*) indicates the absolute oneness of reality or suchness, contrasted here with "myriad dharmas."

4. Butsujubō Myōzen, 1184–1225, studied on Mount Hiei, later becoming Eisai's disciple in Kennin-ji. In 1223, he went to China with Dōgen and others and remained until his death a little over two years later at the T'ien-t'ung shan monastery.

5. Myōan Eisai (also Yōsai), 1141–1215, is regarded as the founder of Rinzai Zen in Japan.

6. Liang-che 両浙: A circuit division that included what is now Chekiang province and adjacent areas. In T'ang and Sung times, the "Five Mountains" or principal monasteries of Chinese Zen were located in this area on both sides of the Chien-tang River and Hangchou Bay. T'ien-t'ung shan was on the eastern side.

7. T'ien-t'ung Ju-ching 天童如浄, 1163–1228.

8. T'ai-pai Peak (T'ai-pai feng 太白峰), another name for the monastery-complex at T'ien-t'ung shan.

9. *Isshō sangaku no daiji* 一生参学の大事; "The greatest matter of religious life." Enlightenment, the ultimate attainment for which Dōgen had devoted himself to a life of Buddhist practice. Dōgen's religious awakening came as he was sitting in the meditation hall of the T'ien-t'ung monastery. According to the biographical record *Kenzeiki*, it occurred when he heard his teacher Ju-ching shout at a sleepy monk, "Zen practice must be casting off body and mind! What can you accomplish by sleeping your time away!"

10. Dōgen actually reached Kyūshū on his way home in the autumn of the previous year, 1227. In 1228, the first year of the She-ting era, he was back home in Kyoto.

without any fixed abode, attempting to transmit through my actions the way of life followed by outstanding Zen masters of the past.

But there will be those who have no concern for gain or glory, authentic religious seekers whose desire for the Way takes precedence over all else. They will be led vainly astray by mistaken teachers, and the right understanding will be arbitrarily obscured from them. They will become needlessly drunk with their own delusions and immersed forever in the world of illusion. How can the true seed of *prajna* be expected to quicken and grow within such seekers? How will they ever reach the moment of attainment? As I am now committed to a wandering life, to what mountain or river can they proceed to find me? It is a sense of pity for the plight of such people that now makes me write down for those who would learn to practice the Way, the customs and standards of the Zen monasteries of great Sung China that I saw with own eyes and have learned and the profound teachings of their masters that I have succeeded to and follow and transmit. I want such seekers to know the right Buddha Dharma. Here are its true essentials.

At an assembly on Vulture Peak, the great teacher Shakyamuni Buddha imparted to Mahakashyapa the Dharma that was subsequently transmitted from patriarch to patriarch down to Bodhidharma.[11] Bodhidharma traveled to China and conveyed the Dharma to Hui-k'e,[12] marking the initial transmission of the Buddha Dharma to eastern lands. It then made its way in direct, personal transmission to the Sixth Patriarch, Ta-chien.[13] By that time, the genuine Buddha Dharma had beyond doubt spread extensively in China. It appeared there with its essence unaffected by any ramifying doctrinal accretions. The Sixth Patriarch had two superior disciples, Huai-jang of Nan-yüeh and Hsing-ssu of Ch'ing-yüan.[14] As possessors and transmitters of the Buddha-seal,[15] they were

---

11. During an assembly on Vulture Peak (Skt: Gṛdhrakūṭa), Brahma, King of the gods, came and implored the Buddha to preach for the benefit of sentient beings. The Buddha held out a lotus flower before the assembly. None of those present could understand his meaning, except Mahakashyapa, who smiled. The Buddha exclaimed, "I have the right Dharma eye, the wondrous Mind of nirvana . . . this I entrust to you Kashyapa." According to the Zen school, this marked the beginning of the Zen transmission.

12. Hui-k'e, the Second Patriarch of Chinese Zen.

13. Ta-chien is one of Hui-neng's posthumous titles.

14. The Five Schools (or Gates) of Chinese Zen, enumerated below, are all offshoots of the teaching lines that stem from Nan-yüeh Huai-jang and Ch'ing-yüan Hsing-ssu.

15. The Zen school, which is also referred to as the "Buddha-mind sect," is said to transmit its essence from mind to mind. A master gives a disciple his *inka* 印可 ("seal of confirmation") when he finds the disciple's mind in complete accordance with his own. The Buddha-seal 佛印 (also mind-seal 心印 or Buddha-mind seal 佛心印) signifies the authentic transmission of the Buddha-mind, and in Sōtō Zen is usually explained as the act of zazen itself, which in all Buddhas is invariably the same.

masters for men and devas alike. Their two schools spread and branched into Five Houses: the Fa-yen, Kuei-yang, Ts'ao-tung, Yün-men, and Lin-chi schools. At present in the great Sung, the Lin-chi school alone is found throughout the country. Although among these Five Houses there are differences to be found, they are all equally based on the one Buddha-mind seal.

Scriptural writings were transmitted to China from the western lands during the Latter Han dynasty.[16] They spread over the empire. But even in China, no determination was reached about which of the various teachings was superior. Following the cxrival of Bodhidharma from the west, these entangling complications were cut away at their source, and the one Buddha Dharma, free from all impurity, began to spread. We must pray that this will take place in our country as well.

It is said that all the patriarchs and Buddhas who have maintained the Buddha Dharma have without question considered practice based upon proper sitting in *jijuyū* samadhi as the right path that led to their enlightenment. All those who have gained enlightenment in India and China have followed in this way of practice as well. It is a matter of rightly transmitting the wonderful means in personal encounter from master to disciple, and on the disciple's sustaining the true essence thus received.

According to the authentic tradition of Buddhism, this personally and directly transmitted Buddha Dharma is the supreme of the supreme. From the first time you go before your master and receive his teaching, you no longer have need for incense-offerings, homage-paying, nembutsu, penance disciplines, or sutra reading. Just cast off your body and mind in the practice of zazen.[17]

When even for a short period of time you sit properly in samadhi, imprinting the Buddha-seal in your three activities of deed, word, and thought,[18] then each and every thing throughout the dharma world is the Buddha-seal, and all space without exception is enlightenment. Accordingly, it makes Buddha-tathagatas increase the Dharma-joy welling from their original source[19] and renews the adornments of the Way of enlightenment. Then, when all classes of

---

16. Latter Han dynasty, A.D. 25–220. In 67, the Indian monks Kashyapa-matanga and Gobharana (Dharmaraksa) arrived in the Chinese capital of Lo-yang, and there translated (or wrote) the *Ssu-shih-erh chang-ching* (Sutra of Forty-Two Sections).

17. In *Hōkyō-ki*, Dōgen noted a similar teaching he received from his teacher Ju-ching: "Commitment to Zen is casting off body and mind. You have no need for incense-offerings, homage-paying, nembutsu recitation, penance disciplines, or sutra readings. Just sit single-mindedly." *Hōkyō-ki*, Ikeda Rosan, ed. section 15.

18. *Sangō* 三業. The three categories of activity, by body, mouth, and mind, that determine karma.

19. The fundamental ground from which Buddha-tathagatas appear; here, the spiritual realm of the *jijuyū* samadhi.

all beings in the ten directions of the universe[20]—hell-dwellers, craving spirits, and animals; fighting demons, humans, and devas—being all together at one time bright and pure in body and mind, realize the stage of absolute emancipation and reveal their original aspects, at that time all things together realize in themselves the true enlightenment of the Buddhas. Utilizing the Buddha-body and immediately leaping beyond the confines of this personal enlightenment, they sit erect beneath the kingly tree of enlightenment, turn simultaneously the great and utterly incomparable Dharma wheel, and expound the ultimate and profound *prajna* free from all human agency.

Since, moreover, these enlightened ones in their turn enter directly into the way of imperceptible mutual assistance,[21] the person seated in zazen without fail casts off body and mind, severs all the heretofore disordered and defiled thoughts and views emanating from his discriminating consciousness, conforms totally with the genuine Buddha Dharma, and assists universally in performing Buddha-work far and wide, at each of the various places the Buddha-tathagatas teach, that are as infinitely numberless as the smallest atom particles—imparting universally the *ki* transcending Buddha, vigorously promoting the Dharma (*hō*) transcending Buddha.[22] Then, with land, trees and grasses, fence and wall, tile and pebble, and all the things in the ten directions performing the work of Buddhas, the persons who share in the benefits thus produced from this wind and water[23] all are imparted unperceived the wonderful and incomprehensible teaching and guidance of the Buddhas, and all manifest their own immediate and familiar enlightenment close at hand. Since those receiving and employing this fire and water all turn round and round the Buddha-making activity of original enlightenment, those who dwell and converse with them also join

---

20. The text has "the ten-direction universe, three paths and six ways," that is, all beings of the universe in all directions (the eight points of the compass, above and below). The *three paths* (*sanzu* 三途) are the Buddhist hells (*jigoku*), the realms of animals (*chikushō*) and craving spirits (*gaki*). The *six ways* (*rokudō* 六道) consist of the above three paths and the realms of the fighting demons (*ashura*), humans, and devas.

21. That is, it is unknowable to human consciousness. The previous paragraph describes the merits one zazen sitting imparts to others. Those merits return to the zazen practicer himself. Dōgen expresses this elsewhere as *dōji jōdō* 同時成道, simultaneous attainment of the Way.

22. Buddhahood means not abiding in Buddhahood but rising beyond the concept and consciousness of Buddha to save others; it does not exist apart from this transcendence. Almost untranslatable, the term *ki* 機, with dictionary equivalents that include spring, trigger, motive principle, potentiality, occasion, and opportunity, is often used with *hō* 法, *ki* referring to the zazen practicer, and *hō* to the changeless Dharma. *Ki* indicates the dynamic Zen function at work in the zazen described in this passage as it turns upon the person sitting, who in doing zazen imparts the *ki* to all things. The Dharma is unchanging, and manifests itself dynamically only when occasion and conditions are ripe.

23. *Wind and water* (and the following *water and fire*) represent the four constituent elements of the material world (*shidai*): earth, water, fire, and wind (or air), which are being spontaneously manifested throughout the phenomenal universe.

with one another in possessing inexhaustible Buddha-virtue, spreading it ever wider, circulating the inexhaustible, unceasing, incomprehensible, and immeasurable Buddha Dharma inside and outside throughout the universe.

Yet such things[24] are not mingled in the perceptions of the person sitting in zazen because, occurring in the stillness of samadhi beyond human agency or artifice, they are, directly and immediately, realization. If practice and realization were two different stages, as ordinary people consider them to be, they should perceive each other.[25] Any such mingling with perceptions is not the mark of realization, for the mark of true realization is to be altogether beyond such illusion.

Moreover, although both the mind of the person seated in zazen and its environment enter realization and leave realization within the stillness of samadhi, as it occurs in the sphere of *jijuyū*, it does not disturb a single mote of dust, or obstruct a single phenomenon,[26] but performs great and wide-ranging Buddha-work and carries on the exceedingly profound, recondite activities of preaching and enlightening. The trees, grasses, and land involved in this all emit a bright and shining light, preaching the profound and incomprehensible Dharma; and it is endless. Trees and grasses, wall and fence expound and exalt the Dharma for the sake of ordinary people, sages, and all living beings. Ordinary people, sages, and all living beings in turn preach and exalt the Dharma for the sake of trees, grasses, wall and fence. The realm of self-enlightenment *qua* enlightening others is originally filled with the characteristics of realization with no lack whatsoever, and the ways of realization continue on unceasingly.

Because of this, when just one person does zazen even one time, he becomes, imperceptibly, one with each and all of the myriad things and permeates completely all time, so that within the limitless universe, throughout past, future, and present, he is performing the eternal and ceaseless work of guiding beings to enlightenment. It is, for each and every thing, one and the same

---

24. That is, the relationships of "imperceptible mutual assistance" described above.

25. The text has "each should perceive the other" (*ono-ono aikakuchi subekinari*), which most commentaries take as a reference to the practice and realization in the previous clause. Since the main concern in the present paragraph is with the functioning of "imperceptible mutual assistance" and the circulation of the Dharma between the zazen practicer and the enlightened things around him, it seems more appropriate to interpret the word *ono-ono* (each . . . the other) as a reference to the Zen practicer and and his "Dharma sphere," the things of the universe. Dōgen mentions the view that practice and realization are two different stages in order to emphasize the contrasting view of "direct realization," in which "imperceptible mutual assistance" occurs without things being "mingled in the perceptions of the one sitting in zazen."

26. Samadhi is not dead stillness without perceptions or consciousness; the mind (perceptions and consciousness) of the zazen practicer and its environment (the sphere of the mind) arise and subside, but do so within the realm of the *jijuyū* samadhi, in which the practicer is one with all things, so this does not result in any disturbance. Cf. *Shōbōgenzō keiteki* I, pp. 86–87.

undifferentiated practice, one and the same undifferentiated realization. Only this is not limited to the practice of sitting alone: the sound that issues from the striking of emptiness is an endless and wondrous voice that resounds before and after the fall of the hammer.[27] And this is not limited to the side of the practicer alone. Each and every thing is, in its original aspect, endowed with original practice—it cannot be measured or comprehended. You must understand that even if all the numberless Buddhas in the ten directions, as countless as the sands of the Ganges, mustered all their might together and by means of Buddha-wisdom attempted to measure and totally know the merit of the zazen of a single person, they could not know the whole of its measure.

## [QUESTIONS AND ANSWERS]

Question 1: You have told us all about the sublime merits of zazen. But an ordinary person might ask you this: "There are many entrances to the Buddha Dharma. What is it that makes you advocate zazen alone?"

Answer 1: Because it is the right entrance to the Buddha Dharma.

Question 2: But why single out zazen alone as the right entrance?

Answer 2: The great teacher Shakyamuni Buddha rightly transmitted zazen as the wonderful means for attaining the Way; all the tathagatas of the three periods attain the Way through zazen as well—which is why they transmit it from one to another as the true entrance. Besides, zazen is how all patriarchs, from India in the west to China in the east, have gained the Way. That is why I now teach it to men and devas as the right entrance.

Question 3: The reason you give, that zazen transmits the Tathagata's wonderful means, which you base upon evidence you trace to the patriarchal teachers, may well be correct—such matters are really beyond an ordinary person's ability to ascertain. For all that, however, surely one can reach enlightenment by reciting sutras and repeating the nembutsu. How can you be certain that if you pass your time sitting idly in zazen, enlightenment will result?

Answer 3: When you characterize the unsurpassingly great Dharma and the samadhi of the Buddhas as merely "sitting idly," you are guilty of maligning the Great Vehicle. It is as profound an illusion as to declare there is no water when you are sitting in the midst of the ocean. Fortunately, the Buddhas are already seated firmly established in jijuyū samadhi. Does that not produce immense

---

27. The merits of enlightenment are realized not only during zazen but also before and after. While zazen is essential for realizing shunyata or emptiness, the fundamental reality of the universe, the working of emptiness is beyond zazen and not affected or produced by it.

merit? It is a pity that your eyes are not opened yet, that intoxication still befogs your mind.

The realm of Buddhas is utterly incomprehensible, not to be reached by the workings of the mind. How could it ever be known to a man of disbelief or inferior intelligence? Only a person of great capacity and true faith is able to enter here. A person who does not believe, even if he is told about such a realm, will find it impossible to comprehend. Even on Vulture Peak, the Buddha told some in the assembly that they might leave.[28] If right faith arises in your mind, you should practice under a master. If it does not, you should cease your efforts for the time being and reflect with regret that you have not been favored with Dharma benefits from the past.[29]

Besides, what do you really know of the merits brought by such practices as sutra-recitation and nembutsu? It is utterly futile to imagine that merely moving your tongue or raising your voice has the merit of Buddha-work. Any attempt to equate those practices with the Buddha Dharma only makes it more remote. Moreover, when you open a sutra to read, it should be for the purpose of clarifying the teachings the Buddha set forth about the rules and regulations for practicing sudden and gradual enlightenment,[30] to convince you that you will attain realization if you follow them. It is not done in order to waste yourself in useless speculation and discrimination, and to suppose that you are thereby gaining merit that will bring you to enlightenment. Intending to attain the Buddha Way by foolishly working your lips, repeating some words incessantly a thousand or ten thousand times, is like pointing the thills of a cart northward when you want to go south, or like trying to fit a square piece of wood into a round hole. To read the Buddha's words while still unaware of the way of practice is as worthless a pastime as perusing a medical prescription and overlooking to mix the compounds for it. If you merely raise your voice in endless recitation, you are in no way different from a frog in a spring field—although you croak from morning to nightfall, it will bring you no benefit at all. Such practices are difficult to relinquish for those who are deeply deluded by fame or profit—this because of the depth of their covetousness. Such people were to be found in ancient times; there is no reason they should not be around today. They deserve our special pity.

---

28. According to the *Lotus Sutra* (Skillful Means chapter), as Shakyamuni was about to preach the difficult and most sublime Dharma teaching at the request of his disciple, Shariputra, an assembly of nuns and monks and lay men and women, 5,000 strong, said they did not wish to hear a teaching different from the one they had hitherto understood, and they began to leave. Shakyamuni did not attempt to stop them, saying that those who wished to leave might do so.

29. That is, from a previous existence.

30. The Buddha is said to have taught two kinds of practice by which people could attain enlightenment quickly or gradually, according to their differing spiritual capacities.

Only make no mistake about this: if a student working under the constant guidance of a clear-minded, truly enlightened teacher realizes his original mind and rightly transmits his Dharma, the wondrous Dharma of the Seven Buddhas[31] is then fully manifested and fully maintained. There is no way for this to be known or even to be approached by a priest who merely studies words. So you should have done with all these uncertainties and illusions; instead, negotiate the Way in zazen under the guidance of a true teacher and gain complete realization of the Buddhas' *jijuyū* samadhi.

*Question 4:* The teachings that are transmitted today in our own Hokke and Kegon schools represent the ultimate Mahayana teaching.[32] Not to mention the teachings of Shingon, which were transmitted personally by Vairochana Buddha to Vajrasattva—they have not been handed down from master to disciple without good reason.[33] Centered in the sayings "the mind in itself is Buddha,"[34] and "this very mind attains Buddhahood," Shingon teaches that the genuine enlightenment of the Five Buddhas[35] is attainable in a single sitting, without having to pass through long kalpas of religious practice. It could perhaps be termed the most sublime point the Buddha Dharma has yet reached. In view of that, what are the advantages of the practice you advocate that you advance it alone and ignore all these others?

*Answer 4:* Be well assured that for a Buddhist the issue is not to debate the superiority or inferiority of one teaching or another, or to establish their respective depths. All he needs to know is whether the practice is authentic or not. Men have flowed into the Way drawn by grasses and flowers, mountains and

---

31. The Seven Buddhas of the Past: Shakyamuni and the six Buddhas that appeared prior to him in the remote past.

32. The Hokke or Lotus school refers to the Japanese Tendai school established by Saichō; in his youth, Dōgen studied at the Tendai monastery on Mount Hiei. Kegon Buddhism, introduced to Japan by Chinese and Korean monks during the Nara period (646–794), was prominent during the Nara and Heian periods.

33. Kūkai, 774–835, also known as Kōbō Daishi, went to China, where he studied under the fourth patriarch of the Chen-yen (真言: Japanese, Shingon) sect, and upon returning to Japan, he founded the Japanese Shingon school. Shingon's chief object of worship is Vairochana, the Great Sun Buddha (Japanese, Dainichi Nyorai, 大日如来). The first Dharma transmission, according to Shingon tradition, was from Vairochana to the Shingon patriarch Vajrasattva, and later through Nagarjuna to Kōbō Daishi.

34. Although our reading, "the mind in itself is Buddha," follows Ōkubo, the earlier "Honzan-ban" text uses the word *body* (*shin* 身) in place of *mind* (*shin* 心), which would seem more appropriate here, since Shingon asserts that attainment of Buddhahood is achieved "in this body" (*sokushin jōbutsu* 即身成仏).

35. In Shingon Buddhism, Dainichi Nyorai 大日如来 is surrounded at the four quarters by four other Buddhas, of which there are two sets, one in the Vajradhātu (Diamond World), another in the Garbhadhātu (Womb-store World).

running water. They have received the lasting impression of the Buddha-seal
by holding soil, rocks, sand, and pebbles. Indeed, its vast and great signature is
imprinted on all the things in nature, and even then remains in great
abundance. A single mote of dust suffices to turn the great Dharma wheel.
Because of this, words like "the mind in itself is Buddha" are no more than the
moon reflected on the water. The meaning of "sitting itself is attainment of
Buddhahood" is a reflection in a mirror. Do not get caught up in skillfully
turned words and phrases. In encouraging you now to practice the immediate
realization of enlightenment, I am showing you the wondrous Way by which
the Buddha-patriarchs transmit the Dharma from one to another. I do this in
the hope that you will become real men of the Way.

Moreover, in receiving and transmitting the Buddha Dharma, it is absolutely essential to have as a teacher a person who is stamped with realization.
Word-counting scholars will not do—that would be a case of the blind leading
the blind. Today, all who follow the right transmission of the Buddha-patriarchs preserve and maintain the Buddha Dharma by following with reverence
a clear-sighted master who has attained the Way and is in accord with
realization. Because of that, the spirits of the realms of light and darkness[36]
come to him and take refuge; enlightened Arhats[37] also seek him out to beg his
teaching. None are excluded from acquiring the means of illuminating the
mind-ground. This is something unheard of in other teachings. Followers of
Buddha should simply learn the Buddha Dharma.

You should also know that basically we lack nothing of highest enlightenment. We are fully furnished with it at all times. But because we are unable to
come to complete agreement with it, we learn to give rise to random intellec-
tions and, by chasing them, supposing them to be real,[38] we stumble vainly in
the midst of the great Way. From these mistaken views appear flowers in the air
of various kinds:[39] thoughts of a twelve-link chain of transmigration, realms of
twenty-five forms of existence, notions of three vehicles, five vehicles, Buddha,
no-Buddha[40]—they are endless. You must not think that learning such notions
is the proper path of Buddhist practice.

---

36. The "spirit realms" (shindō 神道) are the transmigratory realms of devas, fighting demons,
and craving spirits. The "spirits of light" are the devas; the "dark spirits" those of the latter two
realms.

37. Saints who have attained the fourth and highest stage in Theravada Buddhism.

38. Ōkubo has "thinking" (omou 思う) for "chasing" (ou 追う). Here we follow the emenda-
tion in the first printed text of Bendōwa, published in 1788 by Gentō Sokuchū.

39. These are flakes seen by those with eye disease; used in Buddhism to express what is imagi-
nary and without basis in reality.

40. The twelve-link chain of transmigration includes twelve causal links that cause transmigration
through the three worlds of past, present, and future. The twenty-five forms of existence—including

But now, when you cast everything aside by singlemindly performing zazen in exact accordance with the Buddha-seal, at that moment you outstep the confines of illusion and enlightenment, sentiment and calculation and, unbothered by alternatives of unenlightened and enlightened, you stroll at ease beyond the world of forms and regulations enjoying the function of great enlightenment. How can those enmeshed in the traps and snares of words and letters begin to measure up to you?

*Question 5:* Samadhi is one of the three learnings.[41] Dhyana is one of the six paramitas.[42] Both are learned by all Bodhisattvas from the beginning of their religious life and practiced irrespective of a person's mental capacity. The zazen you speak of would seem to be included in these categories. What grounds do you have for stating that the right Dharma of the Buddha is concentrated solely in zazen?

*Answer 5:* Your question arises because the incomparable truth of the right Dharma eye that is the Buddha's great and central concern[43] has come to be called the "Zen sect." Bear this well in mind: the appellation "Zen sect" is found in China and the lands east of China; it was unknown in India. During the nine years that the great teacher Bodhidharma performed zazen facing a wall at the Shao-lin monastery on Mount Sung, the priests and laymen of the time did not yet know the right Dharma of the Buddha. They said Bodhidharma was an Indian monk whose religion consisted of doing zazen. In generations after that all Buddhist patriarchs invariably devoted themselves to zazen. Unthinking people outside of the priesthood, observing this and not knowing the true circumstances, began to speak loosely of a "Zazen sect." At present, the word *za* has been dropped, and people speak of the Zen sect. The essence of the school is made clear throughout the recorded sayings of the Zen patriarchs. It is not to be equated with the samadhi or dhyana included among the six paramitas or three learnings.

Never has there been anything unclear or ambiguous about it. The Buddha himself wanted this Dharma to be his legitimate transmission. Some among

---

fourteen realms of desire, seven realms of form, and four formless realms—are those through which unenlightened sentient beings transmigrate. The *three vehicles* (teachings that bring people to various stages of enlightenment) carry living beings across samsara (birth-and-death) to the shores of nirvana: the shravaka (the hearer), the pratyeka-buddha (the self-enlightened), and the bodhisattva. The *five vehicles* are the three vehicles, plus the human and deva realms.

41. *Sangaku:* the three forms of Buddhist learning: discipline (*śīla*), concentration (*samādhi*), and wisdom (*prajñā*), thought to be the fundamental "studies" every Buddhist practicer must undertake.

42. The six "perfections" (*paramitā*) are practices by which enlightenment is attained: donation, precept-keeping, perseverance, assiduity, meditation, and wisdom.

43. The reason tathagatas appear in the world is to help sentient beings attain salvation.

the deva multitude now present in the heavens actually witnessed the ceremony that took place many years ago during the assembly on Vulture Peak,[44] when the Tathagata entrusted his right Dharma eye, his wondrous mind of nirvana, to Mahakashyapa alone. So there is no reason for any doubt. Without ever ceasing or diminishing their efforts, those deva hosts devote themselves to protecting and maintaining the Buddha Dharma throughout all eternity.

You should just know without any doubt or uncertainty whatever that this Dharma [zazen] is, in its entirety, the all-inclusive Way of the Buddha's Dharma. There is nothing else even to compare with it.

*Question 6:* What grounds are there for Buddhists to emphasize Zen meditation and place so much weight on sitting alone among the four attitudes (moving, standing, sitting, lying)? To say this is the path to entering realization?

*Answer 6:* It is not possible to exhaustively survey the way in which Buddhas, one after another from ages past, have practiced and entered realization. If you must have a reason, you should simply know that this is the way that Buddhists use. Further reasons are unnecessary. Haven't patriarchs extolled zazen as the "Dharma gate of repose and joy," because among the four bodily attitudes it is sitting that affords repose and joy? Remember, this is the way of practice employed not by one Buddha or two, but by all Buddhas and all patriarchs.

*Question 7:* So those who have not yet realized the Buddha Dharma can, by negotiating the Way in the practice of zazen, attain that realization. But what about those who have already achieved realization—what can they expect to gain by doing zazen?

*Answer 7:* Proverbs caution against relating one's dreams to the foolish, or placing boat-poles in the hands of woodsmen. Nevertheless, I will try to explain matters once again.

To think practice and realization are not one is a non-Buddhist view. In the Buddha Dharma, practice and realization are one and the same. As your present practice is practice within realization, your initial negotiation of the Way is in itself the whole of original realization. That is why from the time you are instructed in the way of practice, you are told not to anticipate realization apart from practice. It is because practice points directly to original realization. As it is from the very first realization in practice, realization is endless. As it is the practice of realization, practice is beginningless. Hence both Shakyamuni and Mahakashyapa were brought into the great functioning by practice within realization. Bodhidharma and patriarch Hui-neng were also drawn into the

---

44. The Buddha transmitted his teaching to Mahakashyapa in the presence of a congregation of humans and devas. For the devas known as *trāyastriṃśa* (Japanese, *tōriten*) one year is equal to 500 years in the human realm, making it possible that they are still alive.

functioning by practice within realization. And it has been the same for all those who have maintained the Buddha's Dharma.

It is practice inseparable from the outset from realization, and since fortunately we [practicers] all transmit a portion of wondrous practice ourselves, even our negotiation of the Way as beginners obtains a portion of original realization at a ground that is utterly free of human agency. You should know that in order to keep from defiling this realization that is inseparable from practice Buddhas and patriarchs teach unceasingly that we must not allow our practice to diminish. When we cast off the wondrous practice, original realization fills our hands ; when we transcend original realization, wondrous practice permeates our bodies.

When I was in Sung China, everywhere I went I saw that the Zen monasteries were all built to include a special hall for zazen. Five hundred or 600 monks, sometimes even up to 2,000 monks, were housed in these halls and encouraged to devote themselves to zazen day and night. When I asked the head priests of these monasteries, teachers who transmit the authentic seal of the Buddha-mind, about the essence of the Buddha's Dharma, they told me that practice and realization are not two stages.

For that reason, I urge not only those who come here to practice with me, but all high-minded seekers who aspire to the truth that is found in the Buddha Dharma—whether beginners or experienced practicers, wise sages or just ordinary people—to conform to the teachings of the Buddha-patriarchs, to follow the Way of the true masters, and negotiate the Way in zazen.

Do you know the words of one of those patriarchs? "It is not that there is no practice or realization, only that we must not contaminate them [by attaching to them]."[45] Another said: "Those who are able to see the Way, practice the Way."[46] What you must understand is that your practice takes place within realization.

*Question 8:* In former times, when teachers traveled to China and returned as Dharma-transmitters to spread Buddhism in our country,[47] why did they ignore zazen and transmit only the doctrines?

*Answer 8:* Teachers in the past did not transmit zazen because the circumstances were not yet ripe for it.

*Question 9:* Did the teachers of earlier times understand this Dharma (zazen)?

*Answer 9:* If they had, they would have made it known.

---

45. Nan-yüeh Huai-jang. *CTL*, ch. 5.

46. Pen-ching of Ssu-k'ung shan, 667–761. *CTL*, ch. 5.

47. This probably refers to such teachers as Kūkai and Saichō, mentioned before.

*Question 10:* Some have said: "Do not concern yourself about birth-and-death. There is a way to promptly rid yourself of birth-and-death. It is by grasping the reason for the eternal immutability of the 'mind-nature.' The gist of it is this: although once the body is born it proceeds inevitably to death, the mind-nature never perishes. Once you can realize that the mind-nature, which does not transmigrate in birth-and-death, exists in your own body, you make it your fundamental nature. Hence the body, being only a temporary form, dies here and is reborn there without end, yet the mind is immutable, unchanging throughout past, present, and future. To know this is to be free from birth-and-death. By realizing this truth, you put a final end to the transmigratory cycle in which you have been turning. When your body dies, you enter the ocean of the original nature.[48] When you return to your origin in this ocean, you become endowed with the wondrous virtue of the Buddha-patriarchs. But even if you are able to grasp this in your present life, because your present physical existence embodies erroneous karma from prior lives, you are not the same as the sages.

"Those who fail to grasp this truth are destined to turn forever in the cycle of birth-and-death. What is necessary, then, is simply to know without delay the meaning of the mind-nature's immutability. What can you expect to gain from idling your entire life away in purposeless sitting?"

What do you think of this statement? Is it essentially in accord with the Way of the Buddhas and patriarchs?

*Answer 10:* You have just expounded the view of the Senika heresy. It is certainly not the Buddha Dharma.[49]

According to this heresy, there is in the body a spiritual intelligence. As occasions arise this intelligence readily discriminates likes and dislikes and pros and cons, feels pain and irritation, and experiences suffering and pleasure—it is all owing to this spiritual intelligence. But when the body perishes, this spiritual intelligence separates from the body and is reborn in another place. While it seems to perish here, it has life elsewhere, and thus is immutable and imperishable. Such is the standpoint of the Senika heresy.

But to learn this view and try to pass it off as the Buddha Dharma is more foolish than clutching a piece of broken roof tile supposing it to be a golden jewel. Nothing could compare with such a foolish, lamentable delusion. Hui-chung of the T'ang dynasty warned strongly against it.[50] Is it not senseless to

---

48. *Shōkai* 性海, the essential realm of the true nature, the original source of all phenomena, termed an ocean because it is universal and all-embracing.

49. The Senika heresy (*senni-gedō* 先尼外道), which appeared during the Buddha's lifetime, emphasized the concept of a permanent self. See *Nirvana Sutra*, ch. 39.

50. Nan-yang Hui-chung, 683–769. In *CTL*, ch. 8, Hui-chung cautions a monk against this heresy. The Senika heresy also appears in *SBGZ Sokushinzebutsu.*

take this false view—that the mind abides and the form perishes—and equate it to the wondrous Dharma of the Buddhas; to think, while thus creating the fundamental cause of birth-and-death, that you are freed from birth-and-death? How deplorable! Just know it for a false, non-Buddhist view, and do not lend an ear to it.

I am compelled by the nature of the matter, and more by a sense of compassion, to try to deliver you from this false view. You must know that the Buddha Dharma preaches as a matter of course that body and mind are one and the same, that the essence and the form are not two. This is understood both in India and in China, so there can be no doubt about it. Need I add that the Buddhist doctrine of immutability teaches that all things are immutable, without any differentiation between body and mind. The Buddhist teaching of mutability states that all things are mutable, without any differentiation between essence and form.[51] In view of this, how can anyone state that the body perishes and the mind abides? It would be contrary to the true Dharma.

Beyond this, you must also come to fully realize that birth-and-death is in and of itself nirvana. Buddhism never speaks of nirvana apart from birth-and-death. Indeed, when someone thinks that the mind, apart from the body, is immutable, not only does he mistake it for the Buddha-wisdom, which is free from birth-and-death, but the very mind that makes such a discrimination is not immutable, is in fact even then turning in birth-and-death. A hopeless situation, is it not?

You should ponder this deeply: since the Buddha Dharma has always maintained the oneness of body and mind, why, if the body is born and perishes, would the mind alone, separated from the body, not be born and die as well? If at one time body and mind were one, and at another time not one, the preachings of the Buddha would be empty and untrue. Moreover, in thinking that birth-and-death is something we should turn from, you make the mistake of rejecting the Buddha Dharma itself.[52] You must guard against such thinking.

Understand that what Buddhists call the Buddhist doctrine of the mind-nature, the great and universal aspect encompassing all phenomena, embraces the entire universe, without differentiating between essence and form, or concerning itself with birth or death.[53] There is nothing—enlightenment and

---

51. Immutability and perishability are not separate attributes in the true nature of things. Viewed from the standpoint of immutability, everything is immutable; viewed from the standpoint of perishability, everything is perishable. There is no difference in this respect between mind and body, essence 性 and form 相.

52. Cf. a similar statement below in SBGZ Shōji, p. 106.

53. A similar statement, with slightly different wording, appears in the Daijō-kishinron [Awakening of Faith in the Mahayana].

nirvana included—that is not the mind-nature. All dharmas—the "myriad forms dense and close" of the universe—are alike in being this one Mind. All are included without exception. All those dharmas, which serve as "gates" or entrances to the Way, are the same one Mind. For a Buddhist to preach that there is no disparity between these dharma-gates indicates that he understands the mind-nature.

In this one Dharma [one Mind], how could there be any differentiation between body and mind, any separation of birth-and-death and nirvana? We are all originally children of the Buddha, we should not listen to madmen who spout non-Buddhist views.

*Question 11:* Is it necessary for those who devote themselves to zazen to strictly observe the Buddhist precepts?

*Answer 11:* Observing precepts, pure conduct, is a standard of the Zen school, and a characteristic of Buddhas and patriarchs. However, those who have not yet received the precepts, and even those who break the precepts, are not deprived of the benefits that come from zazen.[54]

*Question 12:* May those who engage in the practice of zazen combine it with the practices of mantra recitation and Tendai *shikan*?[55]

*Answer 12:* When I was in China and had occasion to ask the masters there about the true principle of their schools, they told me they had never heard of any of the patriarchs, those who have rightly transmitted the Buddha-seal throughout the past in India and China, engaging in such combined practices. It is true. Unless you concentrate on one practice, you cannot attain the one [true] wisdom.

*Question 13:* Can lay men and women engage in this practice? Or is it limited to priests alone?

*Answer 13:* The patriarchs teach that when it comes to grasping the Buddha Dharma, no distinction must be drawn between man and woman, high and low.

*Question 14:* Upon entering the priesthood a person immediately sheds the various ties to secular life so there will be nothing to hinder him in his negotia-

---

54. The precepts are all included and present in zazen. "When you are practicing zazen, what precept cannot be observed?" (*Shōbōgenzō zuimonki*, II. 1).

55. We use the word "mantra" to render the word *shingon* 真言 (literally, "true words"), which refers to the mantras and dharanis employed in esoteric Buddhism. These magic or esoteric formulas are repeated to bring various benefits, such as unity with Buddha. *Shikan* 止観 (Skt., *samatha-vipaśyanā*) is a contemplation used chiefly in the Tendai sect which involves cessation of illusory thought and meditation on truth.

tion of the Way in zazen. But how amid the pressures of secular life can he devote himself single-mindedly to such practice and bring oneself into accord with the Buddha Way that is beyond human agency?

Answer 14: Buddha-patriarchs, moved by their great sense of pity for sentient beings, keep the vast gates of compassion open wide. They do this because they want to bring all living beings to realization. There is not a single being, either in the realm of the devas or among mankind, unable to enter. Throughout history we find much evidence to substantiate this. To mention just a few examples: Emperors Tai-tsung and Shun-tsung,[56] though heavily burdened with the myriad affairs of state, negotiated the Way in zazen and penetrated to an understanding of the great Way of the Buddhas and patriarchs.

As imperial counselors serving at the emperor's side, Prime Ministers Li and Fang negotiated the Way in zazen and also realized the great Way.[57] It is simply a question of whether the aspiration is there or not. It has nothing to do with whether one is a layman or a priest. What is more, those who are able to discern the true merits of things come to have faith in the Buddha Dharma naturally. Perhaps I should add that those who think mundane affairs hinder the practice of the Buddha Dharma know only that there is no Buddha Dharma in their daily life; they do not yet know that there is nothing "mundane" in the Buddha Dharma.

A recent minister of the Sung, named Feng,[58] is another high official who excelled in the Way of the patriarchs. In a verse he composed late in his life, he wrote:

> When free from my duties, I practice zazen,
> Rarely do I even lie down for sleep.
> I may appear to be a minister of state,
> But everyone calls me the "elder monk."

Although he could have had little time to spare from the duties of his office, he was possessed of a strong aspiration in the Way, and he attained realization. So you should consider your own situation in the light of others. Look at the present with an eye to the past.

---

56. T'ang dynasty emperors. Tai-tsung reigned in 763–79; Shun-tsung reigned 805.

57. It is unclear who these two officials are. Li may be Li Ao (d. 844), who attained enlightenment under Zen master Yüeh-shan Wei-yen while serving as Prefect of Langchou (CTL, ch. 14). Fang may refer to the official P'ei Hsiu, a student of Huang-po Hsi-yen and compiler of his Zen records.

58. Feng-chieh (d. 1153), lay Buddhist name Pu-ting, achieved enlightenment under Fo-yen Ch'ing-yüan, 1067–1120, and received Dharma sanction from Ta-hui Tsung-kao, 1089–1163.

Today in the land of the great Sung, the emperor and his ministers, those in official positions and ordinary citizens as well, men and women alike, everyone has the Way of the patriarchs constantly in their thoughts. Both soldiers and men of learning aspire to the study and practice of Zen. Many of those who so resolve are certain to awaken to an understanding of the mind-ground. Thus you can readily see that worldly affairs are no hindrance to the Buddha Dharma.

When the authentic Buddha Dharma spreads and is at work throughout a country, it is under the constant protection of the Buddhas and devas. Hence the benevolent rule of the king will be felt by his subjects, and the country will be at peace. Under a benevolent reign, with the country at peace, the influence of the Buddha Dharma is bound to increase.

Moreover, in the time of Gautama Buddha, even transgressors against the Dharma[59] and those holding false views attained the Buddha Way. Among the followers of the Zen patriarchs, there were hunters and fuel-gatherers who attained satori, so is it possible that others would be unable to? But you must seek the guidance of an authentic teacher.

*Question 15:* Is it possible to attain realization by practicing zazen even in this evil, degenerate age of the latter day?

*Answer 15:* While the doctrinal schools make much of names and forms, in authentic Mahayana teaching there is no differentiation between right, semblance, and final Dharma.[60] It preaches that all who practice attain the Way. In fact, in the right Dharma that has been passed down without deviation, you enjoy the precious treasure within your own home[61] the same upon entering it as a beginner as you do when you attain deliverance. Those who practice are themselves aware of their attainment or non-attainment, just as a person knows without any doubt whether the water he is using is warm or cold.

---

59. Those who commit one of the ten evils: killing living beings, theft, adultery, lying, rough speech, duplicitous speech, idle talk, greed, anger, false views; or one of the five cardinal sins: killing one's father or mother, killing a saint, injuring the body of a Buddha, causing disunity in the Sangha.

60. The doctrine of the right, semblance, and final Dharma (*shō-zō-matsu* 正像末), referring to the three periods after the Buddha's death, was especially prominent during the Heian and Kamakura eras. Although there are different views as to the duration of these three periods, according to one prevalent at the time of Dōgen's writing, the first period of the right Dharma was believed to last 1,000 years, during which Buddhist doctrine, practices, and enlightenment all existed; this was followed by a second 1,000-year period of the semblance or counterfeit Dharma, during which doctrine and practices existed but not enlightenment, and a third and final period, the latter or final Dharma, of a 10,000-year duration, during which the doctrine alone remained. Since it was thought that the advent of the final or *mappō* Dharma fell during late Heian times (1052, according to one contemporary estimate), there was a general feeling of pessimism abroad in society that influenced the teachings of evangelists such as Hōnen, Nichiren, and Shinran.

61. The "precious treasure" is the Buddha-nature.

*Question 16:* Some say that if you penetrate fully the meaning of "the mind in itself is Buddha," even though you do not recite scriptures or actually engage in religious practice, you are lacking nothing of the Buddha Dharma. The mere knowledge that the Buddha Dharma inheres within you is the perfect, total attainment of the Way. You should not seek it elsewhere, in any other person. Then what need is there to trouble yourself with negotiating the Way in zazen?

*Answer 16:* Such words are especially meaningless. Were things as you portray them, would not all spiritually perceptive persons be able to arrive at understanding merely by being taught such words?

Understand that the Buddha Dharma consists above all in practice that strives to eliminate views that distinguish self and other. Were the Way attained by knowing your self is Buddha, Shakyamuni would not have troubled himself as he did long ago to lead others to enlightenment. Let me corroborate this with some examples of worthy priests of the past.

A monk of former times named Hsüan-tse was temple steward in the brotherhood of Zen master Fa-yen.[62] Fa-yen said to him, "Tse, how long is it that you've been with me?" "It's been three years now," he answered. "As a member of the next generation, why is it you never ask me about the Buddha Dharma?" Tse replied, "I must not deceive you. Formerly, when I was with Zen master Ch'ing-feng, I attained the Dharma realm of blissful peace." Fa-yen asked, "By what words did you attain that realm?" Tse replied, "I once asked Ch'ing-feng, 'What is the self of a Buddhist disciple?' He answered, 'Ping-ting t'ung-tzu comes for fire.'"[63] "Those are fine words," said Fa-yen. "But you probably didn't understand them." Tse said, "I understand them to mean this: Ping-ting is associated with fire. To look for fire with fire is like looking for the self with the self." "You see," said the master, "you didn't understand. If that were the extent of the Buddha Dharma, it would not have been transmitted to the present day."

Hsüan-tse, indignant, promptly left the monastery. As he was leaving, he reflected, "The master is known throughout the land. He is a great teacher with over 500 disciples. There must be some merit in his admonishment."

He returned penitently to the monastery, performed his bows before Fa-yen, and asked, "What is the self of a Buddhist disciple?" "Ping-ting t'ung-tzu comes for fire," the master replied. On hearing these words, Hsüan-tse attained great enlightenment.

---

62. Fa-yen Wen-i, 885–958, founder of the Fa-yen "House" of Chinese Zen; Hsüan-tse was an heir of Fa-yen.

63. This dialogue appears in *CTL*, ch. 17. There are no dates for Zen master Ch'ing-feng. *Ping-ting t'ung-tzu* 丙丁童子 (Japanese, *hyōjō dōji*), the "fire boy," is a personification of fire.

It is obvious the Buddha Dharma cannot be realized by understanding that "the self is the Buddha." If that were the extent of the Buddha Dharma, the master would not have said what he did to guide Hsüan-tse. He would not have admonished him as he did.

When you encounter a good master for the first time, just inquire about the rules and regulations with regard to practice, and then devote yourself wholeheartedly to negotiating the Way in zazen. Do not let your mind dwell upon superficial or partial knowledge. If you follow this advice, you will not find the Buddha Dharma's wonderful means unavailing.

*Question 17:* In scanning the past and present in India and China, we find that one person was enlightened upon hearing a pebble strike against a bamboo; another's mind was cleared at the sight of blossoming flowers.[64] Indeed, Shakyamuni himself realized the Way when he saw the morning star; and Ananda discerned the truth when a banner-pole fell.[65] From the time of the Sixth Patriarch, a great many other people filiated to the Five Houses of Zen were enlightened by a single word or phrase. Yet did all of those people, to a man, negotiate the Way in zazen?

*Answer 17:* It should be clearly understood that those of the past and the present whose minds were enlightened by seeing things or hearing things all negotiated the Way without any preconceptions whatever; and that for each of them, right at that instant, no "other person" existed.

*Question 18:* In India and China people possess a natural intelligence and uprightness. When people in these centers of culture are taught the Buddha Dharma they are unusually quick to reach understanding and realization. In our country, however, benevolence and wisdom have not existed in abundance. It has been difficult for the right seeds to accumulate. It is indeed regrettable that our backwardness has produced this state of affairs. The priests in our country are inferior to even the laymen in those great lands. A general obtuseness pervades our entire culture, and the minds of our countrymen are small and narrow. People are deeply attached to worldly, material gain, partial to goodness and virtue of a very superficial kind. Even were such people to engage in the practice of zazen, would it really be possible for them to realize the Buddha Dharma?

---

64. This is a reference to the enlightenment experiences of Hsiang-yen Chih-hsien and Ling-yün Chih-ch'in. Hsiang-yen's came when he heard a pebble strike against a bamboo, Ling-yün's upon seeing a flowering peach tree.

65. Shakyamuni is said to have attained enlightenment upon looking up and seeing the morning star. His disciple Ananda was enlightened when Mahakashyapa asked him to take down the banner-pole at the gate.

*Answer 18:* As you say, benevolence and wisdom are still not widespread among our countrymen. Their dispositions are narrow and perverse. Even if the right Dharma, undistorted, were given to them, its ambrosial nectar would likely turn to poison. They are easily moved to seek fame and profit, and so they find it difficult to free themselves from attachment and illusion.

All that is true, and yet in entering into realization of the Buddha Dharma, the ordinary commonsense knowledge of men and devas is not necessarily the vehicle by which the world of illusion is transcended. Even in the Buddha's time, one man realized the four stages to sainthood because of a bouncing ball.[66] The great Way was illuminated for another when she put on a surplice (*kesa*).[67] Both were ignorant, dull-witted people, no more enlightened than beasts, but by virtue of right faith the path of deliverance from illusion opened for them. A laywoman experienced satori while watching a foolish old monk sitting silently as she was serving his meal.[68] It was not the result of wisdom or of culture, and it did not depend upon the spoken word or upon the relating of a story. It was right faith alone that saved her.

Moreover, the spread of Shakyamuni's teaching through the 3,000 world universe took only about 2,000 years. The lands making up this universe are diverse. Not all of them are countries of benevolence and wisdom. Certainly their inhabitants are not all astute and sagacious. Yet the Tathagata's right

---

66. This story is found in the *Tsa-pao-tsang-ching*, ch. 9. An old monk, muddled by age, heard some young monks discussing the four stages to Arhatship and was carried away by the desire to attain them himself. He asked them for instruction, and they jestingly replied that they would oblige him if he treated them to a feast. Having finished their meal, they directed the old man to sit upright in a corner. He joyfully acquiesced, whereupon they began to bounce a ball against his head, saying, "That's the first stage." But with that, the old monk actually did attain the first stage toward his goal. They continued to bounce the ball against his head, each time in a different corner, each time assuring him that he had reached the second, third, and fourth stages, and the monk, each time the ball bounced from his head, did attain each of the stages, including the fourth and highest.

67. The Buddhist nun Utpalavarna (Japanese, Rengeshiki bikuni 蓮華色比丘尼), a disciple of the Buddha, always praised the virtues of the priesthood to everyone she met. She told them of her former life as a courtesan, when she would don various costumes and dance for her customers. One day, running out of ideas, she decided to put on a Buddhist surplice. This led to her entrance into Buddhist life and subsequent attainment of highest enlightenment. The story is found in the *Ta-chih-tu-lun*, ch. 13.

68. A sharp-witted woman who was deeply devoted to Buddhism used to provide food for monks in return for some words on the Dharma. One day a feeble-minded old monk came and partook of a fine meal. The woman expected to receive a sermon as usual, but the witless monk could think of nothing to say, and when she sat down and closed her eyes in anticipation, he grabbed the opportunity and fled. But as she sat waiting, she attained the first stage of Arhatship. Overjoyed, she opened her eyes to find the old monk gone, so she searched him out and thanked him deeply. The monk was so repentant that he too attained the first stage. See the *Tsa-pao-tsang ching*, ch. 9.

Dharma is originally endowed with the strength of incomprehensibly great merit and virtue. When the time comes, the Dharma will spread in a land. If people just practice with right faith, they will all attain the Way, irrespective of the amount of intelligence they possess. Do not think because ours is not a land of great benevolence and wisdom, or because the people's knowledge is small and their understanding feeble, that the Buddha's Dharma cannot be comprehended here. Besides, the right seed of prajna-wisdom exists in abundance in all people. It seems only that, having rarely been in accord with that wisdom, our countrymen have as yet been unable to enjoy its use.

## [EPILOGUE]

The foregoing exchange of questions and answers is not altogether consistent. The standpoints of questioner and replier have sometimes interchanged. How many flowers have been made to blossom in the sky! But in Japan the essential principles of negotiating the Way in zazen have not yet been transmitted. We must pity those who aspire to know them. Therefore, I have collected something of what I saw and heard while I was in China. I have written down the true secrets of the enlightened masters I encountered there so that I could convey them to practicers who might desire to know them. At this time I have not had occasion to go beyond this and describe the standards of behavior in their monasteries, or the rules and regulations I observed in their temples. Such matters do not lend themselves to hurried or casual exposition.

It is true that Japan is a remote land, lying beyond the clouds and smoke to the east of the Dragon Seas. Yet from the time of the Emperors Kimmei and Yōmei,[69] we have been blessed by the gradual west-to-east movement of the Buddha Dharma. However, a disorderly proliferation of doctrinal names and forms and ritual matters has taken place, and there have been difficulties regarding the place of practice as well.

Now as you fashion a hermitage among blue cliffs and white rocks and with mended bowl and tattered robe begin your religious discipline on your own by properly sitting in zazen, the matter transcending Buddha is immediately manifested,[70] and the great matter of a lifetime of practice is forthwith

---

69. Kimmei 欽明 (reigned 539–571). Buddhism is traditionally said to have been introduced into Japan from Korea in A.D. 552 when the King of Paekche presented Emperor Kimmei with a bronze image of Shakyamuni, some sutras, and other religious objects. It was during the reign of Yōmei 用明 (reigned 585–7), Kimmei's fourth son and father of Prince Shōtoku, that Buddhism began to gain favor among the ruling classes.

70. See note 22.

penetrated to ultimate fulfillment.[71] This is the instruction left by Lung-ya,[72] and the style of the teaching bequeathed by Mahakashyapa.[73] The manner and principles of the zazen you practice should be based on the *Fukanzazengi*, which I compiled during the preceding Karoku period.[74]

Although the spread of the Buddha Dharma in a country should await the decree of the king, we need only remember the meaning of the message the Buddha delivered on Vulture Peak to recall that the kings, nobles, ministers, and generals presently ruling innumerable lands throughout the world all humbly received that message and were reborn in their present existence without forgetting the deep desire from their previous existence to protect and maintain the Buddha Dharma.[75] Are not all the regions in which their influence prevails Buddha lands? So it does not necessarily follow that in order to propagate the Way of the Buddha-patriarchs, you must choose a favorable place and wait for ideal circumstances to develop. And you must never think that you are starting new from today.

That is why I have gathered these words together to leave for the wise ones who aspire to the true Dharma, as well as for those true practicers who seek the Way like floating clouds and drifting water-plants.

---

71. See note 9.

72. Lung-ya Chü-tun, 835–923. One of Lung-ya's poems describes the content of his "instruction." "Uncooked food, rude clothing, mind like the full moon; /Throughout life without a thought, without limit. If my contemporaries ask where I live, Tell them the green waters and blue mountains are my home." Dōgen quotes Lung-ya in *Shōbōgenzō zuimonki*, v, 10: "Studying the Way is above all learning poverty. Study poverty, live in poverty, and immediately you are close to the Way."

73. The text has *Keisoku* 鶏足, "Cock Leg," which refers to Mahakashyapa during the period that he lived on Kukkuṭapāda (Cock Leg Mountain) in Magadha performing austerities.

74. *Fukanzazengi* was written in 1227, immediately after Dōgen returned from China. It is translated above, pp. 2–6.

75. In the *Nirvana Sutra*, Shakyamuni entrusts the spread of the Dharma to the patronage of kings, ministers, and others of great influence. He says that the Dharma should be propagated with the help of the king, but that the Buddha's command is prior to that of kings, who have reached that rank in their present existence for the purpose of preserving and transmitting the Dharma.

THREE

# Ikka Myōju
# 一顆明珠

## (One Bright Pearl)

The colophon attached to the fascicle states that it was "delivered at Kannon-dōri Kōshō-hōrin-ji, Uji, Yōshū, the eighteenth day of the fourth month, fourth year of Katei [1238]." Yōshū is an old name for the Yamashiro region where the capital Kyoto was located, so called after the Yung-chou district of ancient China. Kannondōri Kōshō-hōrin-ji is the name Dōgen gave the new temple built for him in 1236 at Fukakusa. A second colophon, probably added when Dōgen later revised the essay, is included in most modern editions. It reads: "transcribed the twenty-third day of the seventh month, the first year of Kangen (1243), in the temple master's quarters at Yoshimine-dera, Shihinosō, Yoshida-gun, Etchū, by the attendant-monk Ejō." Yoshimine-dera was the temple where Dōgen resided while awaiting completion of the Daibutsu-ji (later renamed Eihei-ji). Ejō was a direct disciple of Dōgen.

The title *Ikka Myōju* is taken from the words of Zen master Hsüan-sha Shih-pei of the late T'ang: "All the universe is one bright pearl." Dōgen gives some brief biographical information about Hsüan-sha, describing his entrance into religious life, subsequent practice, and the enlightenment he attained under the tutelage of his teacher, Hsüeh-feng I-ts'un. He then scrutinizes in various contexts the dialogue between Hsüan-sha and a monk in which the above saying appears, examining it word by word, phrase by phrase. The final third of the work is devoted to general comments on the dialogue (Ōkubo, vol. 1, 59–63).

## IKKA MYŌJU

Tsung-i Ta-shih of Mount Hsüan-sha in Fu-chou, great Sung China, this world of suffering, had the religious name Shih-pei.[1] His secular name was Hsieh. Before he entered the priesthood, he was fond of fishing. He drifted in a boat in the Nan-t'ai river like many other fishermen. No doubt he did not even expect the Golden Fish that comes to you unbidden without angling for it.[2]

At the beginning of the Hsien-t'ung period of the T'ang,[3] there arose in him a sudden desire to leave the world. Giving up his boat, he went into the mountains. He was thirty years old. He had awakened to the uncertainty of the transient world and realized the eminence and sublimity of the Buddha Way.

He finally made his way to Mount Hsüeh-feng and placed himself under the guidance of Chen-chüeh Ta-shih, negotiating the Way day and night.[4] One day he took up his traveling pouch and set out down the mountain to complete his training by visiting other teachers around the country. On the way, he struck his toe hard on a rock. Blood appeared, but amid intense pain he had an abrupt self-realization. Saying, "This body does not exist. Where is the pain coming from?" he promptly returned to Hsüeh-feng.

Hsüeh-feng asked him, "What is this mendicant Pei?"

Hsüan-sha replied, "I will never deceive others."

This answer greatly pleased Hsüeh-feng. "Those words could come from anyone," he said. "But no one [but Pei] could utter them." He pressed on. "Mendicant Pei," he asked. "Why haven't you left on your pilgrimage?"

Hsüan-sha replied, "Bodhidharma did not come to the East. The Second Patriarch did not go to the West."

This reply earned special praise from Hsüeh-feng.

Since he had long been a fisherman, even in his dreams Hsüan-sha had seen none of the great multitude of Buddhist sutras and commentaries, but since he put his deep resolve above all else, an aspiration appeared in him that excelled that of his fellow monks. Hsüeh-feng considered him an outstanding monk, praising him as being foremost among all of his students.

Hsüan-sha used cloth of a simple weave for his robe which, as he wore it

---

1. Tsung-i Ta-shih is the honorific title of T'ang Zen priest Hsüan-sha Shih-pei, 835–908. *This world of suffering*: shaba 娑婆 (Sk. *sahā*) refers to the world of birth-and-death.

2. "The Golden Fish that comes to you unbidden" is a metaphor for the sudden and unexpected nature of self-awakening.

3. The Hsien-t'ung period, 860–873. Hsüan-sha would have been twenty-five when the Hsien-t'ung period began.

4. Mount Hsüeh-feng (Hsüeh-feng shan) is in Fu-chou (the modern Fukien province), the place where Hsüeh-feng I-ts'un, 822–908, lived and taught. Chen-chüeh Ta-shih is the title granted to I-ts'un by T'ang Emperor I-tsung.

continuously without change, was pieced together patch upon patch. His underclothing was made of paper, and he also used mugwort cloth.[5] Except for his practice under Hsüeh-feng, he followed no other master. Still, he strove hard and attained the ability to succeed to his master's Dharma.

Upon attaining the Way, he would instruct people with the words, "All the universe is one bright pearl."[6]

*A monk once asked him, "I've heard you have said that all the universe is one bright pearl. How can I gain an understanding of that?"*

*The master said, "All the universe is one bright pearl. What is there to understand?"*

*The next day the master asked the monk, "All the universe is one bright pearl. What is your understanding of it?"*

*The monk answered. "All the universe is one bright pearl. What need is there to understand?"*

*"Now I know," replied Hsüan-sha, "that you are living in the Cave of Demons on Black Mountain."[7]*

The uttering of *All the universe is one bright pearl* first appeared with Hsüansha. Its essence is this: the entire universe is not vast and large, not minute and small, or square, or round; not the mean, not right, not "the lively vigor of leaping fish," not "unbared and distinct all around." Moreover, because it is not birth-and-death, and is not coming and going, it is birth-and-death, and it is coming and going. This being so, it is the past gone from here; it is the present come from here. As for its ultimate negotiation, who is there to ascertain that it is fragmentary, or to perceive it as immovable?

*All the universe* is an unceasing process, pursuing things and making them the self, pursuing the self and making it things. The utterance "separated" in response to [a monk's] "when sensations arise one is separated from wisdom" is a turning of the head or a changing of the face, a laying open of things and a seizing of opportunity.[8] Because of pursuing things and making them the self

---

5. Dried, pounded mugwort stalks were crudely woven and inserted for warmth inside of the outer robe. There is reference made in the *Chuang Tzu* (Lieh Yü-k'ou chapter) to a poor family that made its living weaving articles out of mugwort.

6. *All the universe* is literally "All the ten directions of the universe," that is, the eight points of the compass and the regions above and below them.

7. According to Buddhist mythology, this is a mountain of utter darkness, receiving neither moonlight nor sunlight, inhabited by demons. It is located at the farthest reaches of the universe. As a Zen term, it describes a deluded state of attachment, particularly an attachment to emptiness.

8. This is based on a dialogue in *LTHY*, ch. 25: A monk said, "I've heard that when sensations arise one is separated from wisdom, that when thoughts stir, one is separated from the substance. But what of the time before sensations arise?" The master said, "Separated!"

A turning of the head or changing of the face represents a change in appearance and new aspects of Reality. Sensations and wisdom and illusion and enlightenment are not different but

the universe in its entirety is unceasing. Because its own nature is prior to such activity, it is ungraspable even in the essence of the activity.

*One bright pearl* is able to express Reality without naming it, and we can recognize this pearl as its name. One bright pearl communicates directly through all time; being unexhausted through all the past, it arrives through all the present. While there is a body now and a mind now—they are the bright pearl. That stalk of grass, this tree, is not a stalk of grass, is not a tree; the mountains and rivers of this world are not the mountains and rivers of this world. They are the bright pearl.

*How can I gain an understanding of that?* This utterance makes it seem as though the monk's karmic consciousness is at play,[9] yet it is the manifestation of the great function which is the great law.[10] Proceeding, you can raise up steep foot-high water, foot-high waves; that is, a ten-foot pearl, a ten-foot brightness.

What Hsüan-sha says—a case of uttering an utterance—[11] is *All the universe is one bright pearl. What is there to understand?* This is an utterance whereby Buddha succeeds Buddha, patriarch succeeds patriarch, Hsüan-sha succeeds Hsüan-sha. Were they to try to escape this succession, they would not be without places to escape. But even if they did clearly escape it for a while, the very fact of their utterance is the unmitigated occasion of the bright pearl's manifestation.

*The next day the master asked the monk, "All the universe is one bright pearl. What is your understanding of it?"* This expresses "What I spoke yesterday was the established Dharma. Today I breathe using two [aspects of the Dharma]. Today I speak the unestablished Dharma, thrusting aside yesterday and smiling today."[12]

---

two aspects of the same bright pearl. The master's reply "Separated!" rebuts the monk's dualistic view.

A disciple's presentation of his understanding to his master—"a laying open of things"—and the master's response—"seizing the opportunity"—are also different aspects of one and the same bright pearl.

9. For Dōgen, the question. "How can I gain an understanding of that?" although not free from the working of consciousness deeply rooted in karma (*gosshiki* 業識), is nevertheless the bright pearl.

10. *Manifestation of the great function* (*daiyūgen* 大用現) indicates absolute freedom that is not subject to any law. Dōgen here gives a twist to a well-known teaching phrase of Zen master Yünmen: "The manifestation of the great function knows no laws" 大用現前不存軌則.

11. Throughout *Shōbōgenzō*, Dōgen attaches special significance to the terms *dō-toku* 道得 ("utterance") and *dō-shu* 道取 ("uttering"). The first character *dō* in these compounds implies "uttering or expressing the Dharma truth." *Dō-toku* might be rendered more fully "to be able (to have the capacity) to utter (or express) the Dharma." *Dō-shu*, on the other hand, seems to refer to the actual act of uttering or expressing this Dharma-utterance (Cf. SBGZ *Busshō*, fn. 4).

12. Once, a non-Buddhist asked the World-honored One, "Yesterday what Dharma did you preach?" "I preached the established Dharma." he replied. "Today what Dharma do you preach?"

*The monk answered, "All the universe is one bright pearl. What need is there to understand?"* This, we could say, is mounting the robber's horse to chase the robber. In the case of the old Buddha Hsüan-sha preaching for his disciple's sake, it is a matter of practicing within a creature different from himself. Just turn your light inward and reflect, how many "What is there to understand?" can there be? I might say, provisionally, "seven pieces of cheese." I might say "five bean cakes." But this is the teaching and practice of the northern Hsiang and southern T'an.[13]

Hsüan-sha said, *"Now I know that you are living in the Cave of Demons on Black Mountain."* Be aware that from antiquity the face of the sun and the face of the moon have never changed. Since the sun's face appears with the sun's face, and the moon's face appears with the moon's face, if I say in the sixth month [my name is] "Right Now," that does not mean my name is "Hot."[14]

Hence the reality and beginninglessness of the bright pearl are totally beyond grasp. *All the universe is one bright pearl*—we do not say two pearls, or three pearls. Your whole body is one authentic Dharma eye. Your whole body is the Real body. Your whole body is One Expression. Your whole body is a radiant light. Your whole body is Mind in its totality. When it is your whole body, your whole body knows no hindrance. Everywhere is round, round, turning over and over. Since the pearl's merit is manifested in this way, the Bodhisattvas Kannon and Miroku are, here and now, seeing forms and hearing sounds; old Buddhas and new Buddhas are bodily manifested, preaching the Dharma.

Just then, when the pearl is thus, it hangs suspended in emptiness,[15] it is

---

he then asked. "Today I preach the unestablished Dharma," replied the Buddha. "Yesterday it was the established Dharma. Why is it the unestablished Dharma today?" "Yesterday's Dharma is established. Today's is not" (*LTHY*, ch. 1).

13. There are an infinite number of "What need is there to understand it?" Dōgen might say provisionally five of this or seven of that, but it would still be teaching and practice as the one bright pearl, or as the gold Dōgen alludes to here: "In the southern Hsiang [River] and the northern T'an [River] is gold that fills the land from end to end." *Pi-yen lu*, Case 18.

14. This is based on the following dialogue: Li Ao asked Yüeh-shan, "What is your name?" Yüeh-shan answered, "Right Now." Not understanding, Li Ao went to the head of the temple. "A while ago I asked Yüeh-shan what his name was. He said, 'Right Now.' What is his name?" The temple master said, "Well, [since it's winter], his name is Han" [Han 韓 was Yüeh-shan's secular name as well as a homophone for "cold" 寒]. When Yüeh-shan heard of this, he said, "If that's all he understands of the distinctions between things, if it was summertime he'd probably say my name was 'hot'" (*Wu-teng hui-yüan*, ch. 5). Since the sun's face is itself the one bright pearl, and the one bright pearl is the sun's face, the sun's face is unchangeable. For Yüeh-shan, every time is right now, the right time, the one bright pearl. Hence, to say his name is cold or hot according to the season is to look only at the changing appearances of things and to overlook their true, unchanging aspect, the original nature—the one bright pearl.

15. The *Bodhisattva Necklace Sutra* (*P'u-sa ying-lo ching*) contains a reference to "a priceless pearl hanging suspended in emptiness."

attached within the lining of clothes,[16] it is found under the chin [of dragons],[17] and in the headdresses [of kings][18]—all is the universe-encompassing bright pearl. It is its character to be attached within clothing. Make no utterance that tries to attach it on the surface. It is its character to be found within head-dresses and under dragon jaws. Do not attempt to sport it on the surface. When you are drunk, there is a close friend who will give the pearl to you, and you as well must without fail impart the pearl to a close friend. When the pearl is attached to someone, he is invariably drunk. It being thus, it is the one bright pearl—all the universe. So although its face seems to keep on changing, turn-ing and stopping, it is the same bright pearl. Knowing that the pearl is indeed like this—that itself is the bright pearl. In this way the colorations and con-figurations of the bright pearl are encountered. When it is thus, there is no reason to doubtingly think that you are not the pearl because you perplexedly think, "I am not the pearl." Perplexing thoughts, doubts, and our accepting or rejecting are but passing, trivial notions. It is, moreover, only the pearl appear-ing as a trivial notion.

Should we not cherish the bright pearl? Such infinite colorations and brilliance? Each of the many facets of its radiant variegations contains the merit of the entire universe—who could possibly usurp it? Not a person in the market-place could throw a tile away.[19] Do not be troubled about whether you will fall into the chain of causality in the six paths.[20] Being essentially unobscured from first to last, the pearl is the original face and the enlightened eye.

Yet both you and I, not knowing what the pearl is and what it is not, have had a great many thoughts and non-thoughts about it, which form into fixed, positive notions. But when, thanks to Hsüan-sha's words, it is made known and clarified that even our bodies and minds are from the very first the

---

16. An allusion to a parable in the *Lotus Sutra* (Five Hundred Disciples chapter) about a man who met a rich friend and drank with him until he became drunk and fell asleep. The friend, obliged to leave on official business, sewed a priceless pearl into the lining of the man's robe so he would not want for food or lodging. Not knowing this, the man woke up and set out on a journey. He led a life and endured great privation, only finding out about the pearl when he chanced to meet his friend once again.

17. This alludes to an anecdote in the *Chuang Tzu* (Lieh Yü-k'ou chapter) about a priceless pearl lying in deep water under the jaws of a black dragon.

18. The *Lotus Sutra* (Peace and Happiness chapter) relates the story of a Chakravartin king who awarded precious jewels to the generals who helped him in gaining his empire, but he would never part with the bright pearl in his headdress.

19. Since all things—even the proverbially useless tile fragment—are the bright pearl, they are beyond being accepted or rejected, picked up or thrown away.

20. Reference is to the six realms through which unenlightened beings transmigrate: the realms of hell, craving spirits, animals, fighting demons, humans, and heaven. The question of falling into the chain of causality is the subject of the well-known koan "Po-chang's Fox" (*Wu-men kuan*, Case 2).

pearl, the mind is no longer I. Should anyone be troubled about accepting or rejecting the arising and subsiding [of mind] as being or not being the bright pearl? No. Even when you are perplexed or troubled, those perplexed or troubled thoughts are not apart from the bright pearl. As there are no deeds or thoughts produced by something that is not the bright pearl, both coming and going in the Black Mountain's Cave of Demons are themselves nothing but the one bright pearl.

# FOUR

# Genjōkōan
# 現成公案

## (MANIFESTING SUCHNESS)

*Genjōkōan* was the second fascicle of *Shōbōgenzō* to be written. According to its colophon, it was written in mid-autumn [the eighth month], the first year of Tempuku [1233], for a lay disciple named Yōkōshū of Chinzei (an alternate name for Kyushu), about whom nothing else is known. It has been conjectured that he was an official attached to the Dazaifu, the government outpost located in northern Kyushu that dealt with foreign affairs and national defense.

Many have written about the difficulties, beauty, and unobtainable depths of *Genjōkōan*. Nishiari Bokuzan, an eminent Sōtō teacher of the Meiji era, calling it one of the most difficult of all the fascicles, said, "This is Dōgen's skin, flesh, bone, and marrow. His entire teaching begins and ends with this fascicle . . . the other ninety-five fascicles are all offshoots of this one."

The term *genjō-kōan* is difficult to translate satisfactorily into English. It appears a few times in earlier Zen writings, but in *Shōbōgenzō* Dōgen attached a special significance to it, using it as a technical term and an important concept in his thought. *Genjō*, literally something like "becoming manifest" or "immediately manifesting right here and now," does not refer to the manifesting of something previously not manifested but rather to the *immediate presence* (or presencing) of all things as they truly are in their suchness, untouched by our conscious strivings; their ultimate reality, realized in religious practice. According to *Shōbōgenzō shō*, the earliest commentary on *Shōbōgenzō*, *kōan* indicates both the individuality of things and their absolute equality—"the sameness of their differences, the difference of their sameness." Hence the term *genjōkōan* points to ultimate reality in which all things exist in their distinctive individuality and are at the same time identical in their "presencing" or manifesting of suchness (*Ōkubo*, vol. 1, 7–10).

## GENJŌKŌAN

When all things are the Buddha Dharma, there is illusion and enlightenment, practice, birth, death, Buddhas, and sentient beings. When all things are without self, there is no illusion or enlightenment, no birth or death, no Buddhas or sentient beings. The Buddha Way is originally beyond any fullness and lack, and for that reason, there is birth and death, illusion and enlightenment, sentient beings and Buddhas. Yet for all that, flowers fall amid our regret and yearning, and hated weeds grow apace.[1]

Practice that confirms things by taking the self to them is illusion: for things to come forward and practice and confirm the self is enlightenment.[2] Those who greatly enlighten illusion are Buddhas. Those greatly deluded amid enlightenment are sentient beings.[3] Some people continue to realize enlightenment beyond enlightenment. Some proceed amid their illusion deeper into further illusion.[4]

When Buddhas are truly Buddhas, there is no need for them to perceive they are Buddhas. Yet they are realized, fully confirmed Buddhas—and they go on realizing Buddhahood continuously.[5]

---

1. A similar passage appears in Dōgen's collected sayings: "Flowers fall because of our longing, weeds flourish because of our hatred" (*Eihei kōroku*, ch. 1).

2. Although self and all dharmas (things), enlightenment and illusion are originally one and undifferentiated, within the myriad dharmas in constant flux there are occasions when the self is directed toward things (searching for Buddha externally, outside oneself), which is said to be illusion, and occasions when the self is confirmed by things, which is enlightenment. This is because the former is not, as is the latter, free of the self's conscious strivings. Here Dōgen indicates that oneness is not equality that merely eliminates distinctions. Cf. "The Dharma turns the self: the self turns the Dharma. When the self readily turns the Dharma, the self is strong and the Dharma weak. When, on the other hand, the Dharma turns the self, the Dharma is strong and the self is weak. The Buddha Dharma originally includes both of these" (*Gakudō-yōjinshū*, section 7).

3. Enlightenment and illusion, Buddhas and sentient beings, are inseparable. Illusion means being deluded about enlightenment; enlightenment is being enlightened about illusion.

4. *Realize enlightenment beyond enlightenment* indicates the elimination of the "traces" of enlightenment, mentioned previously. This is *butsukōjōji* 佛向上事, "the matter of going beyond Buddha," not abiding in Buddhahood but transcending it (referred to in *Bendōwa*, p. 20).

5. True Buddhahood is free of the consciousness of Buddhahood. Attainment of Buddhahood is a matter of attaining enlightenment without clinging to it.

Seeing forms and hearing sounds with body and mind as one, they make them intimately their own and fully know them.[6] But it is not like a reflection in a mirror, it is not like the moon on the water.[7] When they realize one side, the other side is in darkness.

To learn the Buddha Way is to learn one's self. To learn one's self is to forget one's self. To forget one's self is to be confirmed by all dharmas. To be confirmed by all dharmas is to cast off one's body and mind and the bodies and minds of others as well.[8] All trace of enlightenment disappears, and this traceless enlightenment continues on without end.[9]

The moment you begin seeking the Dharma, you move far from its environs. The moment the Dharma is been rightly transmitted to you, you become the Person of your original part.[10]

When a man is in a boat at sea and looks back at the shoreline, it may seem to him as though the shore is moving. But when he fixes his gaze closely on the boat, he realizes it is the boat that is moving. In like manner, when a person tries to discern and affirm things with a confused notion of his body and

---

6. *Seeing forms and hearing sounds* is presumably an allusion to the well-known enlightenments of Ling-yün, which occurred when he saw a peach tree in flower, and Hsiang-yen, which came when he heard a pebble strike a bamboo.

7. Most commentaries explain these two similes merely in terms of their dualism. However, it seems more natural to take them as references to the clarity and brightness of the reflection, in which case the paragraph would indicate that one realizes upon attaining enlightenment that things and oneself are one, but it is not that the moon reflected on the water (hearer, seer) receives the total moonlight (Dharma) in all its clarity and brightness, because in this case, "When they realize one side, the other side is darkness." This is the idea of *genjō-kōan* 現成公案 that Dōgen expresses below as "when he attains one dharma, he permeates that one dharma; when he encounters one practice he practices that one practice," and "the moment one's realization is ultimate, it is manifested, but [one's] inherent being is not necessarily [all] manifested." *Shōbōgenzō shō* comments: "When we speak of body and mind, there is nothing apart from body and mind. When we speak of forms and sounds, there is nothing apart from forms and sounds. This is the meaning of "when they realize one side, the other side is in darkness."

8. Cf. *SBGZ Shōji*: "When you let go of body and mind, forgetting them both, and throw yourself into the house of Buddha, and when the functioning begins from the side of Buddha drawing you in to accord with it, then, with no need for any expenditure of either physical or mental effort, you are freed from birth-and-death and become Buddha. There can then be no obstacle in anyone's mind."

9. Although all trace or consciousness of enlightenment disappears with the casting off of body and mind, enlightenment itself does not disappear but continues into your everyday life and then on endlessly. If any trace of enlightenment exists, it is not truly enlightenment or casting off of body and mind.

10. The Dharma is not to be found externally; it is inseparable from oneself, and the self is inseparable from the Dharma. If you seek it elsewhere, you fall into illusion. When you are free from attachment to self and attachment to Dharma, you receive the transmission of the Dharma. As this transmission is a matter of awakening to the Dharma inherent in oneself, Dōgen refers to it elsewhere as "the right transmission from oneself to oneself" (*SBGZ Bukkyō*).

mind, he makes the mistake of thinking his own mind, his own nature, is permanent and unchanging. If he turns back within himself, making all his daily deeds immediately and directly his own, the reason all things have no selfhood becomes clear to him.[11]

Once firewood turns to ash, the ash cannot revert to being firewood. But you should not take the view that it is ashes afterward and firewood before. You should realize that although firewood is at the dharma-stage of firewood, and that this is possessed of before and after, the firewood is at the same time independent, completely cut off from before, completely cut off from after. Ashes are in the dharma-stage of ashes, which also has a before and after. Just as firewood does not revert to wood once it has turned to ashes, human beings do not return to life after they have died. Buddhists do not speak of life becoming death. They speak of being "unborn." Since it is a confirmed Buddhist teaching that death does not become life, Buddhists speak of being "undying." Life is a stage of time, and death is a stage of time. It is like winter and spring. Buddhists do not suppose that winter passes into spring or speak of spring passing into summer.[12]

The attainment of enlightenment is like the moon reflected on the water. The moon does not get wet, and the surface of the water is not broken. For all the breadth and vastness of its light, the moon comes to rest in a small patch of water. The whole moon and the sky in its entirety come to rest in a single dewdrop on a grass tip—a mere pinpoint of water. Enlightenment does not destroy man any more than the moon makes a hole on the surface of the water. Man does not obstruct enlightenment any more than the drop of dew obstructs the moon or the heavens.[13] The depth of the one will be the measure of the

---

11. Dōgen uses the boat analogy to point out the illusion of mistakenly accepting the impermanent as permanent. If you keep your eyes on your "boat" (turn within yourself) and cease to follow external dharmas, you will realize that you and all dharmas are without permanent self and thus awaken from the illusion that your self is permanent. In Bendōwa (Answer 10) Dōgen refutes the so-called Senika heresy, which holds that while the body perishes, the mind-nature or self does not.

12. Considered conceptually, firewood becomes ash in a before-and-after sequence, but as they truly are, in their suchness, firewood is firewood and ash is ash, without any distinction of before and after. The process of becoming is properly understood as the continual "arising and disappearing" (life and death) of the respective "dharma stages" of things.

13. The parallel stated in the first sentence holds throughout the paragraph; the moon is enlightenment, the Dharma; the water is man, the recipient of the Dharma. The metaphor of the moon and the water indicates the unhindered interpenetration of two dharmas. The boundlessness of the moon's light falls to rest on water, on the smallest waterdrop as well as on the vast ocean. The moonlight and the water, having no self to cause obstruction, do not disturb or impede one another. There is complete and utter interpenetration, yet at the same time the moon is the moon and the water is the water.

other's height. As for the time—the quickness or slowness—of enlightenment's coming, you must carefully scrutinize the quantity of the water, survey the extent of the moon and the sky.[14]

When you have still not fully realized the Dharma in body and mind you think it sufficient. When the Dharma fills body and mind, you feel some lack. It is like boarding a boat and sailing into a broad and shoreless sea. You see nothing as you gaze about you but a wide circle of sea. Yet the great ocean is not circular. It is not square. It has other, inexhaustible virtues.[15] It is like a glittering palace. It is like a necklace of precious jewels. Yet it appears for the moment to the range of your eyes simply as an encircling sea. It is the same with all things.[16] The dusty world and the Buddha Way beyond may assume many different aspects, but we can see and understand them only to the extent that our eye is cultivated through practice. If we are to grasp the true and particular natures of all things, we must know that in addition to apparent circularity or angularity, there are inexhaustibly great virtues in the mountains and seas. We must realize that this inexhaustible store is present not only all around us, it is present right beneath out feet and within a single drop of water.

Fish swim the water and however much they swim, there is no end to the water. Birds fly the skies, and however much they fly, there is no end to the skies. Yet fish never once leave the water, birds never forsake the sky. When their need is great, there is great activity. When their need is small, there is small activity. In this way, none ever fails to exert itself to the full, and nowhere does any fail to move and turn freely. If a bird leaves the sky, it will soon die. If a fish leaves the water, it at once perishes. We should grasp that water means life [for the fish], and the sky means life [for the bird]. It must be that the bird means life [for the sky], and the fish means life [for the water]; that life is

---

14. This crux has been explained in various ways. The following is one that seems to be most in keeping with the context. The depth of one drop of water holds the vast heights of the moon and the heavens. Length of time is not crucial; that enlightenment (the Dharma) manifests itself regardless of the length of practice can be seen by examining the fact that the moon in the sky is equally reflected on water surfaces of all shapes and sizes and realizing that its reflection is beyond all such limitations and distinctions.

15. As you proceed forward, you gradually realize the inadequacy of your attainment. As long as you think your grasp of the Dharma is sufficient, you are still attached to it. "The so-called matter of transcending Buddha is attaining Buddha, proceeding, and seeing into Buddha anew" (SBGZ Butsukōjōji). The fullness or lack of the Dharma within you depends on your viewpoint, like an area of water appearing differently to fish, humans, and devas. The word virtue is used here in its original sense of virtus, the inherent power in a person or thing.

16. Based on a commentary on the She ta-ch'eng-lun: "The sea itself basically has no disparities, yet owing to the karmic differences of devas, humans, craving spirits, and fish, devas see it as a treasure trove of jewels, humans see it as water, craving spirits see it as an ocean of pus, and fish see it as a palatial dwelling."

the bird, life is the fish.[17] We could continue in this way even further, because practice and realization, and for all that is possessed of life, it is the same.[18]

Even were there a bird or fish that desired to proceed further on after coming to the end of the sky or the water, it could make no way, could find no place, in either element.[19] When that place is attained,[20] when that way is achieved, all of one's everyday activities are immediately manifesting reality.[21] Inasmuch as this way, this place, is neither large nor small, self nor other, does not exist from before, does not come into being now for the first time, *it is just as it is.*

Because it is as it is, if a person practices and realizes the Buddha Way, when he attains one dharma he penetrates completely that one dharma; when he encounters one practice, he practices that one practice. Since here is where the place exists, and since the Way opens out in all directions, the reason we are unable to know its total knowable limits is simply because our knowing lives together and practices together with the full penetration of the Buddha Dharma.[22]

Do not think that in attaining this place it will ever become your own perception, and be knowable by means of intellection. Although we say the breakthrough into realization is directly and immediately manifested, one's inherent being is not necessarily totally manifested. Doesn't its manifestation have to be so?[23]

As Zen master Pao-ch'e of Mount Ma-yü was fanning himself, a monk came up and said, "The nature of the wind is constancy. There is no place it

---

17. The analogy highlights the dynamic oneness of man and Dharma, practice and enlightenment. "Life" may be said to be the manifesting of ultimate reality (*genjō-kōan*) as non-dualistic oneness—"Life is what I make to exist, and I is what life makes me" (*SBGZ Zenki*).

18. *We could continue in this way even further:* other aspects, in addition to those concerning the dynamic oneness of fish and water, bird and sky, might be mentioned, such as that of practice and realization, which have the same inseparable relation as fish and water.

19. That is, it is a mistake to practice in hopes of achieving the Dharma. For the fish, swimming itself is the Way; for the bird, flying is the Way.

20. That is, the "place" of the fish as it swims; for humans, it is selfless living in which "all things advance forward and practice and confirm the self."

21. Absolute reality is already there, to be manifested through your practice.

22. Another crux given various explanations. The following may be helpful as references. "When just one person does zazen even one time, he becomes, imperceptibly, one with each and all of the myriad things and permeates completely all time. It is, for each and every thing, one and the same undifferentiated practice, one and the same undifferentiated realization. . . . Each and every thing is, in its original aspect, endowed with original practice—it cannot be measured or comprehended" (*Bendōwa*, pp. 13–14).

23. Inherent being (*mitsuu* 密有): the Buddha-nature. Although enlightenment always entails self-awakening, the Buddha-nature, being immeasurable, is not totally manifested to one's consciousness (not graspable by perception) in this awakening.

does not reach. Why use a fan?" Pao-ch'e answered, "You only know the nature of the wind is constancy. You haven't yet grasped the meaning of its reaching every place." "What is the meaning of its reaching every place?" asked the monk. The master only fanned himself. The monk bowed deeply.[24]

Verification of the Buddha Dharma, the authentic transmission of the vital Way, is like this. To say that one should not use a fan because the wind is constant, that there will be a wind even when one does not use a fan, fails to understand both constancy and the nature of the wind. It is because the nature of the wind is constancy that the wind of the house of Buddhism reveals the great earth's golden presence and ripens the sweet milk of the long rivers.[25]

---

24. Pao-ch'e of Ma-yü was a disciple of Ma-tsu. This dialogue is found in *LTHY*, ch. 4. The wind-nature connotes the Dharma-nature or Buddha-nature. The meaning of the monk's question is: Since according to the sutras everyone is possessed of the Buddha-nature, what need is there to practice (use the fan) to attain Buddhahood? It is just because the wind-nature is constant that the wind rises up when the fan is moved. Yet without an actual movement of the fan, the wind's constancy remains a latent and an empty reality. For the disciple to believe the wind would arise without the movement of the fan would be like expecting the Dharma to be manifested in oneself without practice.

25. The "wind of the house of Buddhism" (*butsuke no fū* 佛家の風) refers to the Buddha Dharma or, more precisely in this context, to practice that is itself a "verification" (証) or realization of the Buddha Dharma. Since everything is originally the Buddha Dharma, the great earth is always golden, the long river always sweet milk (*soraku* 蘇酪), but they are seen as such only upon attainment of realization.

# FIVE

# Uji
# 有時

## (Being-Time)

*Uji* was written at the beginning of winter, the first year of Ninji [1240], while Dōgen was teaching at the Kōshō-ji, south of Kyoto. It is one of the central fascicles of *Shōbōgenzō*, and one of the most difficult. In it, Dōgen investigates the normally highly abstract concept of time. Although the subject of time is one not generally encountered in Zen literature, in *Shōbōgenzō Uji* time—or what is the same thing, being-time, being that is inseparable from time—is Dōgen's central theme, and it is present as an underlying theme in the other major fascicles as well. In *Uji*, Dōgen uses his Zen dialectic to scrutinize the various ramifications of time from the basic, non-objectifiable premise that asserts the inseparability of time and being in the instant present of the "I" (*Ōkubo*, vol. 1, 189–94).

Note: In *Uji*, as in some of the other fascicles, the Chinese texts that are the subject of Dōgen's commentary are set in italic type when they first appear *en bloc* at the heads of the various sections.

UJI

> An old Buddha said:
> For the time being, I stand astride the highest mountain peaks.
> For the time being, I move on the deepest depths of the ocean floor.
> For the time being, I'm three heads and eight arms.
> For the time being, I'm eight feet or sixteen feet.
> For the time being, I'm a staff or a whisk.
> For the time being, I'm a pillar or a lantern.
> For the time being, I'm Mr. Chang or Mr. Li.
> For the time being, I'm the great earth and heavens above.[1]

The "time being" means time, just as it is, is being, and being is all time.

The sixteen-foot golden Buddha-body is time; because it is time, it has time's glorious golden radiance. You must learn to see this glorious radiance in the twelve hours of your day.[2] The [demonic ashura with] three heads and eight arms is time; because it is time, it can be in no way different from the twelve hours of your day. Although you never measure the length or brevity of the twelve hours, their swiftness or slowness, you still call them the twelve hours. As evidence of their going and coming is obvious, you do not come to doubt them.[3] But even though you do not have doubts about them, that is not

---

1. In the original Chinese text, the characters u-ji 有時 (literally, being time) which are repeated at the beginning of each line of the quotation, mean aru toki, "at a certain time," "sometimes": first the old Buddha does this, then does that, and so on. Such a reading objectifies time, separating it from being, making it something that comes out of the future and disappears into the past, and being something that exists at a certain limited span within that endlessly extending time. To elucidate the inseparability of time and being, Dōgen reads the characters u-ji individually as "being-time," bringing out a meaning latent in the original words: each "certain time," any and every time, is a direct manifestation of being, and vice versa. The translation "for the time being" attempts to encompass something of these meanings.

The old Buddha is Yüeh-shan Wei-yen. Mountain peaks suggests the aspect of differentiation; ocean depths, undifferentiated sameness or wholeness. Three heads and eight arms is the figure of the ashura or fighting demon, unenlightened existence in general; in contrast to eight feet or sixteen feet, a Buddha, Shakyamuni, in seated and standing attitudes, respectively. Mr. Chang or Mr. Li: Tom, Dick, Harry. The first two lines of the saying appear in CTL, ch. 14, but the quotation as a whole appears to have been cobbled together by Dōgen from various sources in Zen literature.

2. Dōgen's commentary on the quotation begins with the key sentence The time being means, showing the unusual significance he gives to the words u-ji, being time. (Since the original Japanese does not differentiate between singular and plural, being and time can be both singular and plural: e.g., being(s) are all time(s)).

Glorious golden radiance: a Buddha's body, often described as tall and golden-colored and emitting radiant light. Buddhas and their radiance, even the strange figure of the ashura, are all time, not as remote or external appearances but as one's own being-time right here in the immediate present.

3. The twelve hours (in the old horary calculation one day was divided into twelve), that is, time, is something we normally take for granted.

Evidence . . . is obvious: e.g., in the change of seasons.

to say you know them. Since a sentient being's doubting of the many and various things unknown to him are naturally vague and indefinite, the course his doubtings take will probably not bring them to coincide with this present doubt. Nonetheless, the doubts themselves are, after all, none other than time.[4]

We set the self out in array and make that the whole world.[5] We must see all the various things of the whole world as so many times. These things do not get in each other's way any more than various times get in each other's way.[6] Because of this, there is an arising of the religious mind at the same time, and it is the arising of time of the same mind. So it is with practice and attainment of the Way.[7] We set our self out in array, and we see that. Such is the fundamental reason of the Way—that our self is time.[8]

Since such is its fundamental reason, we must study and learn that myriad phenomena and numberless grasses [things] exist over the entire earth, and each of the grasses and each of the forms exists as the entire earth.[9] These comings and goings are the commencement of Buddhist practice.[10] When you have arrived within this field of suchness, it is a single grass, a single form. The forms are understood and not understood, the grasses are grasped and not grasped.[11]

---

4. The nature of an unenlightened person's doubt concerning his own time (being) itself (*this present doubt*). He should call it into question, but even while he does not, and remains in illusion, that does not alter the fact that his doubts, like everything else, are part of being-time.

5. The "self" or "I" is the true self, the self in its suchness. From the standpoint of this self (i.e., as being-time), all things are manifestations of itself; thus what we actually see when we look at the "world" is our self "set out in array." (In *SBGZ Uji*, except where reference is clearly to the unenlightened self, the words "self" or "I" are synonymous with being-time.)

6. For example, a bamboo is a bamboo (or a "bamboo-time") and does not obstruct a pine tree being itself; night is night and does not impede the day. See footnote 61.

7. As the self's being-time is totally independent and complete in itself, and at the same time contains within it the whole world and all time, when the self gives rise to the mind that desires enlightenment (or engages in practice, or attains enlightenment, or anything else), at that very time, in that very being-time, the whole world does as well.

8. Since in the self's time there is nothing that is not the self, nothing apart from the self exists for it to see. To realize this way of seeing is enlightenment—the fundamental truth of the world's suchness.

9. That is, because the self's time is like this, limitless dharmas (various forms and "grasses") are being manifested throughout the world as the self *set out in array*. At that time, each and every one of these dharmas contains the whole world.

10. *Comings and goings* (ōrai 往来) presumably refers here to the manifesting of being-time described above, the dynamic, all is one, one is all relation of forms and grasses, the whole earth, and the self. Practicing with the self of the whole world in this way is the commencement of Buddhist practice.

11. That is, in the realm of attainment, when the self "practices" in concert with the whole world and all dharmas are seen and realized in their true aspect as being-times. Understanding and not understanding this both belong to man's discrimination; they are separate but equally manifestations of being-time.

As the time right now is all there ever is, each being-time is without exception entire time.[12] A grass-being and a form-being are both times. Entire being, the entire world, exists in the time of each and every now. Just reflect: right now, is there an entire being or an entire world missing from your present time, or not?[13]

In spite of this, a person holds various views at the time he is unenlightened and has yet to learn the Buddha's Dharma. Hearing the words "the time being," he thinks that at one time the old Buddha became a creature with three heads and eight arms, and that at another time he became a sixteen-foot Buddha. He imagines it is like crossing a river or a mountain: the river and mountain may still exist, but *I* have now left them behind, and at the present time *I* reside in a splendid vermilion palace. To him, the mountain or river and I are as distant from one other as heaven from earth.[14]

But the true state of things is not found in this one direction alone. At the time the mountain was being climbed and the river being crossed, I was there [in time]. The *time* has to *be* in me. Inasmuch as I am there, it cannot be that time passes away.[15]

As long as time is not a modality of going and coming, that time on the mountain is the immediate present—right now—of "the time being" (being-time). Yet as long as time takes upon itself a modality of going and coming, the *being* in me in the immediate *now* of "the time being" is being-time.[16] So does not the time climbing the mountain or crossing the river swallow up the time of the splendid vermilion palace? Does not that time spit out this time?[17]

---

12. That is, there is only the immediate present, in which all time and being is encompassed. This is true of me and of all other dharmas as well.

13. It is not of course missing from any "now." Dōgen is exhorting students to make the truth of being-time their own realization. Without this realization, being-time is a hollow phrase, and they are cut off from the whole world and all time—the authentic mode of being-time.

14. This paragraph presents the ordinary view of time. *In spite of this*—the fact that all time and being are included in the present now. *Creature with three heads and eight arms* (*sanzu happi* 三頭八臂), illusion, contrasted to *sixteen-foot Buddha* that follows. Likewise, crossing rivers and mountains suggests the path of practice leading to enlightenment. The unenlightened view, with its dualistic understanding of self and things as permanent, independent entities, would thus see practice and enlightenment merely as different stages and time as something that comes out of the future and disappears into the past.

15. Time not only passes (and even then it is not separate from the self) but is at the same time abiding right here in me at each and every instant present, and in each of those points of my being-time the other times are included. While my instant present is always one point or stage in time's passage, that one point always includes all other points past and future.

16. Since being-time is both coming and going and not coming and going, it does not pass, and past time (on the mountain) and all other times are always right here in the present. And yet it does pass, and the time on the mountain (which was my time: "I was there") and the present time (which is also my time: "I am never separate from time") are still both here and now in me.

17. Any time (being) always contains a principle of self-affirmation (in which all other times

The creature with three heads and eight arms is yesterday's time. The sixteen-foot Buddha is today's time. Nonetheless, the nature of the truth of this yesterday and today lies in the time when you go directly into the mountains and look at the myriad peaks around you—hence there is no passing away. So even that three-headed, eight-armed creature makes a passage as my being-time. Although it might seem as if it were somewhere else far away, it is the time right now. The sixteen-foot Buddha-body also makes a passage as my being-time. Although it might seem as if it were somewhere else over there, it is the time right now.[18]

Hence, pine trees are time. So are bamboos. You should not come to understand that time is only flying past. You should not only learn that flying past is the virtue inherent in time. If time were to give itself to merely flying past, it would have to leave gaps.[19] You fail to experience the passage of being-time and hear the utterance of its truth, because you learn only that time is something that goes past.

The essential point is: every entire being in the entire world is each time an [independent] time, even while it makes a continuous series. Inasmuch as they are being-time, they are my being-time.[20]

Being-time has the virtue of seriatim passage.[21] It passes from today to tomorrow, passes from today to yesterday, passes from yesterday to today, passes from today to today, passes from tomorrow to tomorrow, this because passing

---

are negated) and a principle of self-negation (in which other times are affirmed). The time on the mountain swallows (negates) the time of the fine palace and spits it out (affirms, manifests it). The self-identity of this contradiction is always present in the being-time of the present now.

The present time swallows all past time and being and all future time and being and also spits it out. Hence, there is a constant merging of past and future in the present.

18. Although creature and Buddha (and by extension ignorance and enlightenment) are yesterday and today, they are not different. According to the analogy of self and mountain peaks (the world), where the self is (seeing itself set out as the world of diverse and limitless forms), there always is the instant present. Hence, the world with all of its times and beings past and future passes in me as the being-time of my immediate now.

19. If time were merely flying past, there would be no unifying principle of the present, and thus "gaps" (*kangeki* or *kengyaku* 間隙) everywhere.

20. All beings in the universe exist as time; time is their "true face." For me and for each of these limitless being-times existing as the world, the world is "my" being-time. The clause *they are my being-time* これ吾有時なり (which alludes to the series of statements of Yüeh-shan in the opening quotation: *For the time being I stand*, etc.) can therefore also imply the following meanings: I am being-time. They are being-time in me. I have time (e.g., to stand, to move, etc.).

21. The movement of time in its authentic sense as being-time occurs without ever leaving the instant present, as a continuous occurrence of "nows" manifesting themselves discontinuously as independent stages. This *seriatim passage* (*keireki* or *kyōraku* 経歴, also translated simply "passage"), taking place on the standpoint of being-time, is thus a discontinuous continuity of such stages (below called "dharma dwelling-stages"), each of which is cut off from "before" and "after," and independent of other being-times while including them all in itself.

seriatim is a virtue of time.[22] Past time and present time do not overlap or pile up in a row—and yet Ch'ing-yüan is time, Huang-po is time. Ma-tsu and Shih-t'ou are times too. Since self and other are both times, practice and realization are times.[23] "Entering the mud, entering the water" is time as well.[24]

Although the views the ordinary, unenlightened person now holds and the conditions that cause them are what the unenlightened person sees, it is not the unenlightened person's Dharma; it is only the Dharma temporarily causing him [to see that way].[25] Since he learns that this time, this being, is not the Dharma, he supposes the sixteen-foot golden Buddha-body is not himself. His attempts to escape by saying, "I am not the sixteen-foot golden Buddha-body" are, as such, portions of being-time as well.[26] It is the "Look! Look!" of "those who have not confirmed this yet."[27]

The horses and sheep now arrayed throughout the world are each dharma stages dwelling in their suchness and moving endlessly up and down.[28] Rats are time. So are tigers. Sentient beings are time, Buddhas as well. This time realizes the entire world by being a creature with three heads and eight arms, and realizes the entire world by being a sixteen-foot golden body.

---

22. In seriatim passage, being-time moves at will in total, unrestricted freedom throughout all time and being. Cf. the paragraph above beginning "The creature . . . is yesterday's time."

23. Each of these Zen masters (it is perhaps significant that the order in which they are cited is not chronological) is being-time (e.g., when Ch'ing-yüan is being-time, he embraces all the others and at the same time is distinct from them (they do not get in each other's way). Similarly, Ch'ing-yüan's practice and realization are each being-time, separate yet identical.

24. *Entering the mud . . . water* (nyūdei nyūsui, 入泥入水): a Zen term usually referring to the work the enlightened undertake upon attaining realization, "entering the world of defilements" to lead the unenlightened to salvation.

25. As the Dharma, in manifesting all things, does not "fall" into distinctions such as enlightened and unenlightened, there can be no question of an "unenlightened Dharma" apart from it. One commentator adds here that nonenlightenment or enlightenment is a matter of whether or not one "obscures" the reality of being-time.

26. Nothing is apart from being-time, even the ordinary person's unenlightened discriminations (e.g., that he and Buddha are different). Still, he ought to strive to realize the truth of himself as being-time.

27. An allusion to words from the *Lin-chi lu:* "In your lump of red flesh is a True Man of no rank [= the I as being-time] who is always coming in and out of your face. For those who have not yet confirmed him, *Look! Look!*" *Those who have not confirmed this yet* refers to "one who attempts to escape" in the preceding sentence. He is a "true man" (*sixteen-foot golden Buddha-body*) but has yet to confirm it.

28. *Horses and sheep* apparently refer to the 12 zodiacal animals (jūnishi) of the sexagenary cycle, which was used to designate the 12 parts ("hours") of the day. *Moving endlessly up and down* refers to the movement of these animals in the daily cycle, as well as to the continuous activity of being-time.

*Dharma (dwelling) stages* (jūhōi 住法位) refers to independent stages or points of being-time, each entire in itself, and ever present in the immediate now. The idea that each dharma dwells independently in its own all-encompassing dharma position.

Entirely worlding the entire world with the whole world is thus called *penetrating exhaustively.*[29] To immediately manifest the bodying of the tall golden Buddha with the body of the tall golden Buddha as the arising of the religious mind, as practice, as enlightenment, as nirvana—that is being, that is time.[30] One does nothing but penetrate exhaustively entire time as entire being. There is nothing remaining left over. Because any dharma left over is as such a leftover dharma, even the being-time of a partial exhaustive penetration is an exhaustive penetration of a partial being-time.[31] Even a form [of understanding] that appears to be blundering is being. On a still broader plane, the times before and after one immediately manifests the blunder are both, along with it, dwelling positions of being-time. The sharp, vital quick of dharmas dwelling in their dharma-positions is itself being-time.[32] You must not by your own maneuvering make it into nothingness; you must not force it into being.

You reckon time only as something that does nothing but pass by. You do not understand it as something not yet arrived. Although our various understandings are time, there is no chance for them to be drawn in by time.[33] There has never yet been anyone who supposed time to be coming and going who has penetrated to see it as being-time dwelling in its dharma-position.[34] What chance is there, then, for a time to arrive when you will break through the barrier [into total emancipation]?[35] Even if someone did know that dwelling-position, who would be able truly to give an utterance that preserved what he

---

29. Time (= being, the creature, the Buddha, etc.) realizes or manifests the entire world as itself (*sets itself out in array*). Nothing is left out of this exhaustive reciprocal interpenetration of all dharmas; no room exists for subject/object dichotomy.

30. The stages of a Buddha's career, each of which is a being-time in which all other Dharma stages are contained.

31. Although nothing is left out as being-time exhaustively penetrates entire time as entire being, an unenlightened man might think he is not this being-time (i.e., that something is left out of his being). But everything is being-time; even his partial being-time is total in terms of itself. So when we blunder or make a mistake in regard to being-time, the blunder is, as such, a time, and is in that sense "being"-time.

32. Sharp, vital quick: *kappatsupatchi*. An onomatopoeic description of the lively movement of a leaping fish, it is often used to describe outstanding Zen activity. Here, it stands for what is utterly ungraspable and unclassifiable into distinctions such as nothingness and being, impermanence and permanence.

33. *Not yet arrived* (*mitō* 未到) also means "not yet understood," or "failure to understand," hence the clause *do not understand it . . . not yet arrived* also has an underlying sense of "do not understand it as itself [= as being-time]."
Even though a person's understanding is not apart from time (= being), the nature of discriminatory understanding is such that it contains no potential cause whereby it may be drawn by being-time into true understanding of that fact.

34. The four sentences beginning *There has never* reflect deepening stages of attainment.

35. That is, to live in complete freedom; free from Dharma dwelling-stages and being-time as well.

had thus gained? And even were someone able to utter such an utterance at will, he could still not avoid groping to make his original face immediately present.[36]

Left entirely to the being-time of the unenlightened, both enlightenment and nirvana would be being-time that was nothing more than an aspect of going-and-coming. [But] no nets or cages remain for long—all is the immediate presencing here and now of being-time.[37] The deva kings and deva multitudes actually presencing to the left and right are even now being-time that puts forth my total exertion. And everywhere else in the universe the hosts of being-times in water and on earth are now immediately manifesting themselves in the full power that I exert.[38] Entities of every manner and kind being time in the realms of darkness and light are all the immediate manifestation of my full exertion, all my full exertion making a passage. One must learn in practice that unless it is one's self exerting itself right now, not a single dharma or thing can either immediately manifest itself or make a passage.[39]

You must not construe this passing to be like a squall of wind and rain moving from place to place. The entire world is not changeless and immoveable, nor unprogressing and unregressing—the whole world is passing seriatim. Passing seriatim is like spring, for example, with all of its many and varied signs. That is passing seriatim.[40] You should learn in practice that passing takes place without anything extraneous. For example, springtime's passage invariably passes through spring. The passage is not spring, but as it is the springtime's

---

36. Even supposing someone could express his fundamental attainment at will, it would still fall short of the total attainment in which his entire activity totally manifests his true self (being-time) as the world and all time.

37. This seems to mean that in spite of the unenlightened view that would make being-time merely an aspect of coming-and-going (without the pivotal ever-present), the entire world is always immediately manifesting itself in the present as being-time totally unencumbered by "nets and cages" (the various mind-made limits and restrictions our illusions construct around us) of any kind.

38. The various forms of existence or being appearing everywhere in the universe appear, and can only appear, as my being-time totally (with nothing left out) exerting itself.

39. The time-by-time (instant-by-instant) manifestation of my being in the instant present includes all other dharmas, just as I am included in the being-time of all other dharmas. Without this interaction of reciprocal interpenetration, nothing can pass or, what is the same thing, be manifest.

40. Although the seriatim passage of the whole world is not a movement from one place or time to another, neither is the whole world devoid of movement. The passage of being-time (the I as the whole world and all time) is like the "career" of springtime passing through as the world. "Spring" is the name provisionally given to the great many diverse signs (birds singing, flowers blooming) which are manifest then and at no other time. (By the same token, when spring passes there is nothing that is not spring.) "Springtime" is the totality of those various signs, and without them spring does not exist; when the signs disappear and others are manifest, we say it is "summer."

passage, passing attains the Way now in the time of spring.[41] All of this you must give careful and repeated examination.

If, in speaking of a "passage," you imagine that the place of passage lies somewhere outside, and the dharma of the one doing the passage moves toward the east [like the spring] through 100,000 worlds over 100,000 kalpas of time, that is a result of not giving total devotion to the single-minded practice of the Buddha Way.[42]

*Once Yüeh-shan Hung-tao, at the direction of Wu-chi Ta-shih, went to Zen master Ma-tsu with a question.*[43] *"I believe I have a fair grasp of the three vehicles and the teaching of the twelve divisions,*[44] *but what about the meaning of the First Patriarch's coming from the west?"*

*Ma-tsu said:*

> *For the time being,*[45] *I let him raise his eyebrows and blink his eyes.*[46]
> *For the time being, I don't let him raise his eyebrows and blink his eyes.*
> *For the time being, my letting him raise his eyebrows and blink his eyes is correct*[47]
> *For the time being, my letting him raise his eyebrows and blink his eyes is not correct.*

*When Yüeh-shan heard this, he achieved great enlightenment. He told Ma-tsu, "When I was at Shih-t'ou's, it was like a mosquito on an iron bull."*[48]

---

41. At the time of spring's passing or "career," there is nothing that is not spring. That does not mean passing is limited only to spring, but merely that the passage of spring is spring realizing itself now or manifesting itself now as itself and as nothing else.

42. The same false view of time as the "going and coming" encountered previously. There is an allusion to the Buddhist idea that long kalpas of practice are needed before Buddhahood can be attained (or the need of many years of zazen to become a Buddha) which, as ordinarily understood, is an objective, dualistic view inimical to authentic Buddhist practice.

43. Wu-chi Ta-shih is an honorific name of Shih-t'ou Hsi-chien. Yüeh-shan Hung-tao 藥山弘道 is Yüeh-shan Wei-yen.

44. That is, all aspects of Buddhist doctrine.

45. For the time being (*uji*). Here Dōgen gives these words the same significance he did in the opening quotation.

46. *Let him raise his eyebrows and blink his eyes*: the Japanese *kare* 伊, translated *him*, can be a personal pronoun or a demonstrative pronoun. Here *kare* apparently refers to Bodhidharma, the first Chinese Zen Patriarch, or to the meaning of his coming.

47. *Correct* (*ze* 是, which may also be translated *is*, *yes*, or *affirmation*) and *not correct* (*fuze* 不是, *is not*, *no*, *negation*) are both being-times, so the sense here does not necessarily involve any relative judgment. For an example of the way *ze* and *fuze* are used in Zen, see the dialogue in Case 31 of the *Pi-yen lu*.

48. The full episode (in *LTHY*, ch. 19), relates how Yüeh-shan went first to study with Shih-t'ou but was unable to make head nor tail of anything he said.

What Ma-tsu utters is not the same as other men.[49] Here eyebrows and eyes must be mountains and seas, because mountains and seas are eyebrows and eyes.[50] Within this "letting him raise," you should see mountains. Within this "letting him blink," you should essentiate the sea.[51] "Correct" enters into intimate terms with "him." "Him" is ushered in by "letting."[52] "Not correct" is not "not letting him," and "not letting him" is not "not correct." All of them are equally being-time.[53]

Mountains are time, and seas are time. If they were not time, there would be no mountains and seas. So you must not say there is no time in the immediate now of mountains and seas. If time is destroyed, mountains and seas are destroyed. If time is indestructible, mountains and seas are indestructible. Within this true dharma, the morning star appears, the Tathagata appears, eye-pupils appear, the holding up of the flower appears.[54] This is time. If it were not time, things would be not-so.[55]

Zen master Kuei-sheng of She-hsien, a Dharma descendent of Lin-chi and direct Dharma heir of Shou-shan,[56] once instructed the assembly of monks:

> For the time being, the mind reaches but the word does not.
> For the time being, the word reaches but the mind does not.
> For the time being, the mind and word both reach.
> For the time being, neither mind nor word reach.[57]

---

49. That is, since they were spoken by Ma-tsu, they must have far deeper meaning and should thus be deeply scrutinized. Dōgen proceeds to direct his remarks to that deeper meaning.

50. *Mountains and seas* suggest (intentionally or not) the mountains and seas in the first quotation. Some commentators see in the way *eyebrows "rise above"* eyes an incidental resemblance to mountains overlooking the sea.

51. The phrase *essentiate the sea* (*umi o shū subeshi* 海を宗すべし) is an attempt to duplicate an unusual verbal form in the original.

52. In this paragraph and the next, Dōgen holds up, from the standpoint of being-time, various aspects of the totally exhaustive reciprocally interpenetrating relation of all times and beings. (This is reflected, for example, in locutions such as *eyebrows and eyes must be mountains and seas, enters into intimate terms with, ushered in by,* and so forth.)

53. *Not correct* and *not letting him* are equally being-time, thus in *not correct's* being-time everything is "not correct" (there is no *not letting him*). The same is true of *not letting him's* being-time.

54. According to Zen legend, Shakyamuni attained Tathagatahood upon seeing the morning star; after his enlightenment, he devoted himself to guiding others to salvation (as in the famous episode when he held up a flower. See page 10, footnote 11). According to the basic principle of being-time, each manifestation appears as itself; when it does, all others appear with it.

55. That is, without the truth of being-time, nothing could come to manifestation, hence, there could be no path of Buddhist emancipation.

56. She-hsien Kuei-sheng, c. 1000, a disciple of Shou-shan Sheng-nien, fourth generation from Lin-chi. The quotation appears in *LTHY*, ch. 20.

57. *For the time being* (see footnote 1, page 48). *The mind reaches but the word does not* 意到句不 到. This forms a set with the following three statements (with many parallels in Zen literature), referring to realization and the utterance or articulation of realization. It should be mentioned that

Mind and the word are equally being-time. Their reaching and not-reaching alike are being-time.[58] Even when the time of their reaching is not yet over, the time of their not-reaching has arrived. The mind is a donkey, the word a horse, making the horse a word and the donkey the mind.[59] "Reaching" is not coming; "not-reaching" is not yet. This is how being-time is.[60]

Reaching is impeded by reaching and not impeded by not-reaching. Not-reaching is impeded by not-reaching and not impeded by reaching.[61] The mind impedes the mind and sees the mind, word impedes word and sees word, impeding impedes itself and sees itself.[62] Impeding impedes impeding—that is time. Although impeding is employed by other dharmas, there has never yet been impeding that impedes another dharma.[63] The entire world, exhaustively, with no thing or time left out, is impeding. I encounter a man. A man encounters a man. I encounter myself. Going forth encounters going forth.[64] If they do not obtain the time, it cannot be thus.[65]

---

the character for "reaches" (*tō* 到) can by extension have a meaning of *coming to fulfillment or attainment.*

58. In the reality of being-time, mind and word are not separate. The following story is sometimes cited to elucidate the relation of reaching (attainment) and not-reaching and being-time: Two monks visited Chao-chou. He asked one of them: "Have you come [reached] here before?" "I've never come before," he replied. Chao-chou said: "Have a cup of tea." Then he asked the second monk the same question. "I've come before," he answered. Chao-chou said: "Have a cup of tea." A senior monk said: "Why did you give them the same response?" Chao-chou said: "Have a cup of tea."

59. An allusion to the following story. A monk asked: "What is the essence of the Dharma?" Master Ling-yün said: "The donkey's not yet gone, and the horse arrives" (*CTL*, ch. 11).

60. Since reaching and not-reaching are both being-time, it is not a question of something that ought to "reach" (arrive or be fulfilled) failing to do so; nor does not-reaching mean something that will eventually reach has not done so yet.

61. *Impeding* (*ge* 礙) is analogous to self-affirmation, the manifesting of true subjectivity. Hence, impeding, which as itself (being-time) is the entire world and all time, signifies the affirming and maintaining of individuality or "selfness," without which there would be a one-sided fall into undifferentiated oneness.

62. When impeding manifests itself, the entire world with no thing or time left out is impeding, thus *it sees itself.*

63. *Although impeding is employed by other dharmas,* for example, a horse is a horse and a donkey is a donkey (each impedes itself and thus manifests itself), hence although a horse's time (being) is all time and all being including the donkey, at the same time the donkey (and all other dharmas) is also all time and being, including the horse. In this way, impeding is "employed" (*shitoku seraru,* 使得せらる) by each dharma, that is, used to maintain its individuality.

Yet that does not mean impeding impedes other dharmas. Impeding only impedes itself, never anything else; if it were otherwise, no other dharma could exist or be manifest (and thus by impeding itself could not exist). There would then be only the one-sided aspect of sameness, and the aspect of difference also vital to the basic standpoint of Buddhism would be lacking.

64. All of these relations are based on being-time's basic standpoint of difference-is-sameness, sameness-is-difference. There is an allusion here to the following story: San-sheng said: "When I encounter men, I go forth. Going forth is not for their sake." Hsing-hua said: "When I encounter men, I do not go forth. Going forth is for their sake" (*LTHY*, ch. 10).

65. That is, nothing is apart from time.

Moreover, the mind is the time of the immediately present ultimate Dharma. The word is the time of the key to higher attainment. Reaching is the time of the body of total emancipation. Not-reaching is the time "you are one with this and apart from this."[66] You should attest and affirm thus. You should being-time thus.[67]

We have seen above how the respected elders have both spoken. Yet is there not something even further to utter?[68]

We should say:

> Half-reaching of mind and word is also being-time.
> Half not-reaching of mind and word is also being-time.

Your investigation must go on like this.

> Letting him raise his eyebrows and blink his eyes is a half being-time.
> Letting him raise his eyebrows and blink his eyes is a "Wrong! being-time.
> Not letting him raise his eyebrows and blink his eyes is a half being-time.
> Not letting him raise his eyebrows and blink his eyes is a "Wrong!" "Wrong!" being-time.[69]

Such investigations continuing in thoroughgoing practice—reaching here and not reaching there—that is the time of being-time.

---

66. These four Zen phrases all indicate ultimate attainment in being-time. Manifesting suchness, or immediately present (*genjō-kōan* 現成公案); the key to higher attainment (*kōjō kanrei* 向上關捩); body of total emancipation (*dattai* 脱体); one with this and apart from this (*sokushi rishi* 即此離此). "When Po-chang returned to Ma-tsu, Ma-tsu said nothing and just took up his whisk. Po-chang said: 'Are you one with that function, or apart from it?' Ma-tsu said nothing and placed the whisk in its original position. After a while, Ma-tsu asked Po-chang: 'How do you preach the Dharma?' Po-chang said nothing and took up the whisk. Ma-tsu said, 'Are you one with that function, or apart from it?' Po-chang said nothing and put the whisk back. At that instant Ma-tsu gave a deafening roar. Po-chang came to final and complete emancipation."

67. Here Dōgen uses *being-time* as a verb, *uji subeshi* 有時すべし.

68. In expressing his own utterances here, Dōgen takes the statements of Ma-tsu and Kuei-sheng even further to assert once again how nothing is apart from being-time.

69. The word *half* in this quotation may be understood in a sense analogous to the word *partial* above (footnote 31). "Wrong" or "mistake" (*shaku* 錯) is more or less analogous. Cf. *Pi-yen lu*, Case 98, T'ien-p'ing's Two Wrongs.

# SIX

# Busshō

# 仏性

(BUDDHA-NATURE)

*Busshō* was delivered at the Kōshō-ji in the tenth month of 1241. *Busshō* is the longest of the fascicles and came to be regarded in the Sōtō school, along with *Genjōkōan* and *Bendōwa,* as one of the three central fascicles of *Shōbōgenzō.* In it, Dōgen takes the central Mahayana Buddhism position that sentient beings all possess the Buddha-nature and the possibility of attaining Buddhahood and gives it his own interpretation from his characteristic, radical, nondualistic perspective.

Perhaps the most striking feature of his treatment of the theme is the clear priority he gives to religious meaning over grammatical syntax, often reading the passages he quotes from various texts in ways that are, in strictly grammatical terms, dubious at best. He does this to focus attention on what he feels are inadequacies in the traditional ways the texts are read and to rectify those inadequacies based on his own understanding. A good example of this is found at the beginning of the work, in his interpretation of a passage from the *Nirvana Sutra* (explained in footnote 1 below).

Like the *Ikka Myōju* and *Uji* fascicles, *Busshō* breaks naturally into a number of sections, each of which commonly begins with a koan or other quotation from Chinese Zen literature, and is followed by Dōgen's Japanese commentary. We have italicized these Chinese texts in the present translation. In order to clarify the difference between the normal reading of these Chinese texts and

Dōgen's interpretative reading of them, we have translated the passages as they would normally be read when the italicized quotation first appears *en bloc* at the beginning of the various sections; then, when Dōgen begins his phrase-by-phrase examination of the quotation, we have given it in a different translation, designed to show as closely as possible the meaning he is attributing to it. The discrepancies between the two readings are explained in the footnotes (*Ōkubo*, vol. 1, 14–35).

## BUSSHŌ

*Shakyamuni Buddha said, "All sentient beings without exception have the Buddha-nature. Tathagata abides forever without change."*[1]

This is the lion roar of our great teacher the Buddha preaching the Dharma. It is also the headtops of all Buddhas and patriarchs, the pupils of all Buddhas' and patriarchs' eyes.[2] Commitment to its study has continued for two thousand one hundred and ninety years (until now, the second year of Ninji), a direct, undeviating lineal descent of exactly fifty generations (until my late master, priest T'ien-t'ung Ju-ching). It has continued uninterrupted for twenty-eight successive generations in India and twenty-three successive generations in China.[3] The Buddhas and patriarchs in the ten directions of the universe have all steadily maintained it.

What is the essence of the World-honored One's words, *All sentient be-*

---

1. Quotation of a well-known passage from the *Nirvana Sutra*, ch. 27. Here it is translated the way it would normally be read: *All sentient beings without exception have the Buddha-nature* (*issai shujō shitsuu busshō* 一切衆生悉有佛性). In his commentary on the passage, however, Dōgen interprets this to mean: "All beings/entire being is the Buddha-nature." He does this by arbitrarily reading the characters *shitsuu* (above, "without exception have") as "entire being." (He is aided by the fact that the character *u* 有 can mean "to be," or "being," and "have".) This changes the idea of sentient beings having a Buddha-nature to stress a standpoint more in keeping with the basic (nondualistic) Mahayana standpoint—entire being *is* the Buddha-nature—in which "entire being" encompasses not only sentient beings but all beings. This avoids a duality of subject (sentient beings) and object (Buddha-nature), a duality that regards Buddha-nature as a potentiality to be actualized in the future, and a duality of means and end (practice the means, realization of Buddha-nature the end). The reading "*entire being is the Buddha-nature*" indicates the nondualistic oneness of realizer (entire being) and realized (Buddha-nature), the simultaneity of Buddha-nature and enlightenment (Buddha), and the identity of practice and attainment. This reading then becomes a key to understanding the various aspects of Buddha-nature that Dōgen develops in the rest of the work.

2. *Headtops . . . pupils*: concrete expressions descriptive of the nonobjectifiable essence of Zen monks.

3. According to the colophon Dōgen appended to *SBGZ Busshō*, he delivered the work the second year of the Ninji period [1241]. Dōgen follows the *CTL*, in calculating Shakyamuni's death date as 949 B.C. It is twenty-eight generations from Shakyamuni to Bodhidharma; twenty-three generations from Bodhidharma to Dōgen's Chinese master Ju-ching.

*ings without exception have the Buddha-nature?* It is his utterance of the Dharma teaching:[4] "What is this that thus comes?"[5] Whether you speak of "living beings," "sentient beings," "all classes of living things," or "all varieties of living beings,"[6] it makes no difference. The words *entire being [shitsuu]* mean both sentient beings and all beings.[7] In other words, *entire being* is the Buddha-nature:[8] I call the whole integral entity of *entire being* "sentient beings."[9] Just at the very time when things are thus, both inside and outside of sentient beings are, as such, the *entire being* of the Buddha-nature.[10] *Entire being* is not only the skin, flesh, bone, and marrow directly transmitted from Bodhidharma to his disciples, for "You attain my skin, flesh, bone, and marrow."[11]

You must understand that the "being" that the Buddha-nature makes

---

4. *Utterance* (*dō-toku* 道得), a Zen term indicating a verbal expression or an articulation of ultimate reality. (See SBGZ *Ikka Myōju*, note 11.)

5. *What is this that thus comes?* Words spoken by the Sixth Patriarch Hui-neng to Nan-yüeh Huai-jang. When Nan-yüeh went to visit Hui-neng, he was asked, "Where have you come from?" "From Sung-shan," he replied. "What is this that thus comes?" asked Hui-neng. Nan-yüeh answered, "The moment I said it was 'this,' I'd miss the mark completely." Hui-neng said, "Then should one engage in practice and realization, or not?" "It is not that there is no practice and realization," said Nan-yüeh, "only that they must not be defiled." Hui-neng said, "It is precisely this non-defiling that all Buddhas retain in mind. You are thus now. I am thus too" (*CTL*, ch. 5). "What is this that thus comes?" is like asking "What is your Buddha-nature?" and thus indicates the manifestation of Buddha-nature itself beyond any predication or definition.

6. These are different terms for sentient beings.

7. *Shitsuu* 悉有: whole, entire being. In the passage quoted above from the *Nirvana Sutra*, these words are normally read "all have [the Buddha-nature]," or, in our translation "[all] without exception have." In Sino-Japanese, the word *u* 有 can mean "being(s)", "to be," as well as "to have," "to possess." Dōgen changes the normal reading of the passage to avoid the dualistic notion of the Buddha-nature as a potentiality to be actualized, or that it is something existing within, and different from, sentient beings. *All beings*: that is, including all sentient and nonsentient beings.

8. *Entire being is the Buddha-nature* (*shitsuu wa busshō nari* 悉有は佛性なり). A key statement. See footnote 1.

9. *Whole integral entity* (*isshitsu* 一悉). In this context, *isshitsu* is usually explained as referring either to a part of entire being or to entire being as a whole. We have thought it best to translate it as "whole integral entity" to avoid the sense of "one" as simply a portion, or the total sum, of entire being. *Isshitsu* conveys the idea that although sentient beings are one form of whole being (*shitsuu*), they at the same time manifest it *totally*.

10. *Inside and outside*. Virtually the same as "self and environment" below (footnote 13).

11. An allusion to the following story. Bodhidharma asked his four disciples what they had attained. The first stated his understanding, and Bodhidharma said, "You have attained my skin." The next two spoke in turn, and Bodhidharma said to one, "You have attained my flesh," and to the other, "You have attained my bone." The last was Hui-k'e, who bowed three times and then stood up. "You have attained my marrow," said Bodhidharma. Hui-k'e subsequently became his successor (*CTL*, ch. 3). Dōgen treats this story in more detail in SBGZ *Kattō*. (*Ōkubo*, vol. 1, 332–33). The allusion to Bodhidharma's words in the present context also emphasizes the essential encounter, face-to-face (e.g., "What is this that thus comes"), that is involved in the Dharma transmission to sentient beings.

*entire being* is not the being of being and nonbeing. *Entire being* is a Buddha's words, a Buddha's tongue, the pupils of a Buddha-patriarch's eyes, the noseholes of a Zen monk. Nor does the term *entire being* mean emergent being, or original being, or mysterious being, or anything of the like, much less conditioned being or illusory being. It has nothing to do with such things as mind and object, substance and form.[12]

Because it like this, the self and surrounding environment of sentient beings-*entire being* is not in the least involved in the waxing influences of karma, is not bred by illusory causation, does not come into being naturally, and is not practiced or realized through miraculous powers. Were sentient being's *entire being* contingent on the power of karma or on causes or on coming into being naturally, then the realization of all saints and the enlightenment of all Buddhas and the eye-pupils of Buddhas and patriarchs also would be produced in these ways—and they are not.[13]

The entire world is completely free of all objective dust; right here and now there is no second person![14] That is because we are unaware that the root source of our illusion is severed, and our busily engaged and widely ranging karmic consciousness [inseparable from the Buddha-nature] never ceases.[15]

---

12. In this paragraph, Dōgen stresses that being the Buddha-nature makes entire being ("just when things are thus" in the preceding paragraph) is nondual and cannot be objectified or in opposition to nonbeing. It is the actual living, functioning being of each Buddha and patriarch; his words and the tongue that speaks them (a Buddha's "long, broad tongue" is said to reach the limits of the universe), his eye-pupils and the life-breathing nostrils of Zen monks. It is not the being of such concepts as emergent being *shiu* 始有 (being that appears in time), *honnu* 本有, original being (absolute, immutable being), and it is not even *myōu* 妙有, wondrous being, which might be described as a kind of synthesis of *shiu* and *honnu*, that is, absolute, essential being manifested as temporal being. Nor is it being that is dependent upon causes or conditions (*en'u* 縁有), or being that is the product of illusion (*mōu* 妄有), illusory being, and it has nothing to do with dichotomous ideas such as mind and object, substance and form.

13. In this paragraph, Dōgen says that *self and surrounding environment* (*eshō* 依正), according to the nondualistic nature of "sentient beings-entire being" (*shujō-shitsuu*) described above, is free of the snowballing influence of karmic cause and effect (*gōzō-jōriki* 業増上力). It neither originates in false and illusory thoughts (*mōengi* 妄縁起), nor is it manifested naturally and spontaneously (*hōni* 法爾), nor attained and realized by means of supernatural powers (*jinzū-shushō* 神通修証).

*Were . . . entire being.* Here "sentient beings' entire being" does not refer to unenlightened sentient beings but sentient beings as identical to Buddha-nature.

14. The reason is given why sentient beings-whole being has no relation to any of the concepts mentioned in the previous paragraph. In the world of entire being, no "dusts" or objects of perception exist that could work upon a subject (*kakujin* 客塵). Each sentient being is at the same time entire being. Here, at that time, there is only the one absolute entire being and thus no "second person" (*dainin* 第二人).

15. This sentence would normally bear a negative connotation: one does not know that the root source of illusion is severed so one's karmic consciousness continues busily functioning, but Dōgen reads it in an affirmative sense: one is prior to knowing (and actually is living) the fact that the root source of illusion is originally severed; the busily working karmic consciousness is as such

This is not being that is bred by illusory causation, because "nothing throughout the whole world has ever been concealed." To say nothing throughout the whole world has ever been concealed certainly does not mean that the world full of being is nothing but being. The idea that the entire world and everything in it are my personal possessions is a false, non-Buddhist teaching.

It is not original (timeless) being, because it fills the past right on up through the present. It is not emergent being, because it does not receive even a particle of dust. It is not separate, individual beings, because it is an all-inclusive whole. It is not beginningless being, because, "What is this that thus comes." It is not being that appears at a certain time, because "my everyday mind is the Way."[16] You must know with certainty that within *entire being* it is impossible, even with the greatest swiftness,[17] to encounter sentient beings. Understood in this way, *entire being* is in itself completely and totally emancipated suchness.

A great many students of Buddhism, when they hear the word Buddha-nature, mistake it for the self expounded by the Senika heresy.[18] That is because they have not encountered a [true] man, they have not encountered their [true] self, they have not encountered an [authentic] teacher. They unwittingly mistake the wind and fire movements[19] of their conscious mind for the enlightenment and awakening of the Buddha-nature. But who has ever said the Buddha-nature is possessed of enlightenment or awakening? Although

---

the manifestation of the Buddha-nature. The karmic (or activity) consciousness, *gosshiki*, denotes the activity of the unenlightened mind in a state of ignorance, and the original, negative sense of the passage suggests that while one is ignorant (unaware) that one is essentially severed from illusion, the karmic consciousness continues working. Dōgen, speaking from the nonobjective standpoint of the absolute person, asserts that one is free from the awareness that one is severed from illusion, is actually living in this state, and the unceasing activity of the karmic consciousness in itself is the activity of the Buddha-nature, the true mode of sentient being-entire being. Such a standpoint does not allow any "second person."

16. Sentient beings-entire being, though appearing in time, is originally free from all sense perception: "the entire world is completely free of all objective dust." It is absolute and eternally changeless and, at the same time, it appears in time. It is not a being of individual entities, because it is at the same time total being; it is not a timeless, eternal being without beginning, because it is *right here*. Yet neither is it a being that begins at a particular point in time, because the Way, the true mode of being (Buddha-nature/entire being) and the everyday mind of suchness are one.

17. *Even with the greatest swiftness*: with sentient beings-entire being objectification is not possible: you cannot encounter sentient beings within entire being because they are not different. All sentient beings exist on the ground of "What is this that thus comes."

18. The Senika heresy (*Senni-gedō*), which appeared in India during the Buddha's lifetime, stressed the existence of a permanent self (see *Bendōwa*, footnotes 49, 50).

19. *Wind and fire movements* refer to discriminations by the sense organs and consciousness of the phenomenal universe in which various mental activities are understood as manifestations of the working of the four great elements (*shidai*)— earth, water, fire, wind—that constitute the universe.

enlightened and awakened beings may be Buddhas, the Buddha-nature itself is neither enlightenment nor awakening. Much less is the "awakening" used in referring to Buddhas as awakened beings the awakening such people indicate with their various mistaken views; and it is not the movement or the stillness of wind and fire. The face of a Buddha, the face of a patriarch—that, and nothing else, is awakening.[20]

It has often been the case that venerable worthies of the past—from the Han dynasty through the T'ang dynasty, and on up until the Sung—men who have travelled to India, who have been teachers to men and devas, as numerous as grain or grass, have believed the wind and fire movements of human consciousness to be the great awakening of the Buddha-mind. It is a terrible pity that their study of the Way was so lax and inadequate as to cause them to make such a mistake.

Advanced students and beginners in the Buddha Way, you must not make this same mistake now. Even if you may study awakening, awakening is not the wind and fire movements of the conscious mind. And even if you study the wind and fire movements of the conscious mind, they are not what you conceive them to be. If you could understand the wind and fire movements of the conscious mind as they truly are, you would also be able to understand true awakening.

With "Buddha" and "nature," if you penetrate one, you penetrate the other: Buddha is nature, nature is Buddha. Buddha-nature is always *entire being*, because *entire being* is the Buddha-nature. *Entire being* is not an infinite number of miscellaneous fragments, nor is it like a single, undifferentiated steel rod. It is a raised fist,[21] so it is neither large nor small. Inasmuch as *entire being* is the Buddha-nature, it cannot be compared to a Buddhist sage. It cannot be compared to the Buddha-nature itself.

There is a certain group that thinks the Buddha-nature is like a seed from a grass or a plant.[22] When this seed receives the nourishment of Dharma

---

20. Although one learns or studies awakening, true awakening is not the working of the conscious mind. Cf. "To learn the Buddha Way is to learn one's own self, to learn the self is to forget the self" (*SBGZ Genjōkōan*). This paragraph criticizes the Senika understanding of religious awakening. In the Senika teaching, the terms *enlightenment* or *awakening* (our translation of the Japanese *kakuchi kakuryō* 覚知覚了) would involve the function of an immutable "spiritual intelligence" residing in man's mutable body. Dōgen rejects the Senika identification of mind with an eternal self that has an existence apart from the mutable body, and he stresses the realization of *total mutability*, the selflessness of all things including body and mind. This realization is in itself the realization of the Buddha-nature—the selfless self, without substance or form.

*True face*: Each Buddha and each patriarch has his own "true face" that manifests entire being, and that is "enlightenment" in its authentic sense.

21. A *raised fist* also has the force of "What is this that thus comes," the absolute "what" being manifested right here (footnote 42).

22. *Seeds from a grass or a plant*: This paragraph and the following refute the idea of the Buddha-

rain, it begins to sprout; branches and leaves, flowers and fruit, appear, and the fruit contain seeds within them.

This supposition is bred from illusion in the unenlightened mind. Even if you yourself should hold such notions, you still should penetrate in practice to the truth that seed and flower and fruit are each, individually, the unbared [Buddha-] mind itself. Fruits contain seeds, and while the seeds cannot be seen, from them the seeds, roots, stem, and the rest of the plant emerge. Although they are not brought together from elsewhere, the twigs and branches develop and multiply, and the main trunk takes form. This is not a result of something inside of the tree or something outside of the tree. Since it always happens the same way throughout past and present, even were we to accept the views of the unenlightened, the roots, stem, branches, twigs, and leaves are each equally the Buddha-nature—living the same life and dying the same death as the same *entire being*.

Buddha said, "*If you wish to know the Buddha-nature's meaning, you must contemplate temporal conditions. If the time arrives, the Buddha-nature will manifest itself.*"[23]

*If you wish to know the Buddha-nature's meaning* is not merely a question of knowing. It means also "if you wish to practice it," "if you wish to realize it," "if you wish to expound it," "if you wish to forget it." This expounding, practice, realization, forgetting, and including such other matters as mistaking it or not mistaking it are temporal conditions.

The way to contemplate temporal conditions is through temporal conditions themselves. It is contemplating temporal conditions of such things as a fly-whisk (*hossu*) or a staff. They can never be contemplated by illusory knowledge, nonillusory knowledge, or knowledge gained in original awakening, initial awakening, nonawakening, or right awakening.

---

nature as a potentiality to be actualized as the result of a process of practice, the "end" or "fruit" of which was alone identified with realized Buddha-nature. For a similar idea, see *SBGZ Genjōkōan*, p. 63.

23. Dōgen devoted the previous section to the *being* of entire being-Buddha nature. Here he deals with *time* and temporal conditions—being and time considered as Buddha-nature. The quotation in a slightly altered form is found in *LTHY*, ch. 7, where it is spoken by Zen master Po-chang Huai-hai. Po-chang cites it from a sutra, presumably the *Nirvana Sutra*, although it is in fact only a loose paraphrase of a passage in that sutra. In our translation, the initial italicized block quotation shows how the passage is normally read. Dōgen rejects that reading, presumably because it would suggest that the Buddha-nature is something potentially inherent in sentient beings that they must actualize through religious practice. Dōgen reads the passage (shown in his phrase-by-phrase treatment of the quotation below) to reveal the nondualistic standpoint in which Buddha-nature and sentient beings, practice and realization, are identical.

Since seeing temporal conditions directly through temporal conditions alone is the realization of the Buddha-nature, there is no need for illusory and nonillusory knowledge, or even for the various wisdoms inherent in enlightenment.

*Must contemplate* has nothing to do with someone contemplating or with something contemplated. It has no correspondence to "right" contemplation or to "false" contemplation. It is just contemplating. Hence, it is not the self contemplating, and it is not another person contemplating. It is "Look!!! temporal conditions!!!" It is the Buddha-nature's emancipated suchness. It is "Look!!! Buddha! Buddha!!!" It is "Look nature!! nature!!!"[24]

Frequently, people of past and present have read the words *If the time arrives* to mean "await a future time when the Buddha-nature might be manifested." "If you continue your practice in such a way," they say, "the time of the Buddha-nature's manifestation will come naturally. If that time does not come, whether you study the Dharma with a teacher, or negotiate the Way in concentrated practice, it will not be manifested." Holding such a view, they return fruitlessly into the world's red dust and gaze vainly up at the non-Buddhists who hold that all comes about spontaneously, as a matter of natural course.[25]

*If you wish to know the Buddha-nature's meaning* might, for example, be read, "Right now you know the Buddha-nature's meaning." *You must contemplate temporal conditions* means "right now you know temporal conditions." If you wish to know the Buddha-nature, you must realize that it is nothing other than temporal conditions themselves.

The utterance *If the time arrives*[26] means "The time is already here, and there can be no room to doubt it." Even if you doubt that the time has arrived [and thereby the Buddha-nature], you may do so, but then "Return the Buddha-nature to me."[27]

---

24. *Must contemplate* (tōkan 当観). Although in this context the normal reading of the character *tō* in the compound *tō-kan* would be "must," Dōgen reads it to mean "just," "immediately," "directly," with *tōkan* becoming "just contemplate, " or "directly contemplate" to avert the dualistic notion of someone watching or waiting for something, and of regarding the present as merely a means or process in reaching some future point.

The word "Look!!!" in this section renders the word *ni* 聻 (or *nii*), an almost untranslatable particle that in normal Zen usage is used to direct attention to the thing that precedes it and to convey with great emphasis (expressed here by multiple exclamation points) the need to grasp the thing directly, as it is in itself. Dōgen uses it to draw attention to what is immediately present here and now—"What is this that thus comes." "Buddha with Buddha!!!" points to the immediate and absolute presence of each and every Buddha, Buddha together with Buddha.

25. *All comes about spontaneously, as a matter of natural course* (Tennen gedō, 天然外道), a heretical doctrine criticized by Buddhists for denying the teaching of cause and effect. It would imply that enlightenment comes without the need for religious practice.

26. *If the time arrives* (jisetsu nyakushi 時節若至) indicates how the Chinese characters *jisetsu nyakushi* would normally be translated; but Dōgen, reading the character *nyaku* as "already" instead of "if" (*nyaku* does have some such meaning, albeit rare: Morohashi *Daikanwa jiten*, 9928b), interprets them to mean "the time is already here."

27. *Return the Buddha-nature to me* (genga busshō rai 還我仏性来). Here the text assumes the

As for *If the time arrives*, you should know that throughout the twenty-four hours of the day no time passes without its already being come.

If it arrives is the same as saying "is already arrived." If the time is already here, the Buddha-nature does not have to come. Hence, the time being already arrived is in itself the immediate manifestation of the Buddha-nature. Or, "This truth is clear and self-evident."[28] There has never yet been a time not arrived. There can be no Buddha-nature that is not Buddha-nature manifested right here and now.

*The Twelfth Patriarch Ashvaghosha, in expounding the "Buddha-nature Sea" for the sake of the Thirteenth Patriarch, said: "The forming of mountains, rivers, the great earth itself, is totally dependent on the Buddha-nature. Samadhi and the six supernatural powers are being revealed through the Buddha-nature."*[29]

In this way, mountains, rivers, and the great earth are all the Buddha-nature Sea. *The forming of mountains, rivers, the great earth itself, is totally dependent* means that the very time they are being formed is mountains, rivers, and the great earth. As for *the forming is totally dependent on the Buddha-nature*, you should know that the mode of the Buddha-nature Sea is like this. It is not concerned with inner or outer or in-between.[30] As the Buddha-nature Sea is like this, seeing mountains and rivers is seeing the Buddha-nature. Seeing the Buddha-nature is seeing a donkey's jowls or a horse's mouth.[31] You understand,

---

character of a Zen dialogue. The teacher says that the student's doubting of the Buddha-nature is fine, since doubting is also the Buddha-nature, but for the time being the student should hand the Buddha-nature over to him, for safe keeping. (Perhaps there is a playful allusion here to words of the Buddha, about a gift that has been rejected reverting to the giver.) Returning the Buddha-nature to him would in any case be a matter of the Buddha-nature returning the Buddha-nature to itself.

28. *This truth is clear and self-evident* 其理自彰. These are words uttered by Po-chang in the original Chinese quotation from *LTHY*, cited above (footnote 23), although when Dōgen dealt with that quotation he changed the words to "Buddha-nature will manifest itself" 佛性現前 (or, as he interprets this to mean, "Buddha-nature is immediately manifested," or "the immediate manifestation of the Buddha-nature").

29. From *CTL*, ch. 1. The Thirteenth Patriarch is Kapimala.

30. *The forming is totally dependent on the Buddha-nature* does not connote dependence in terms of a subject-object duality. Just as the forming of waves is totally dependent on the sea, and the sea does not exist without the waves, the forming of each individual thing is dependent on the ocean of Buddha-nature, and Buddha-nature does not exist apart from individual things. Given this nondualistic relation, formation is itself Buddha-nature, is mountains, rivers, and so on. Mountains, rivers, and so on and the Buddha-nature are two names for one and the same dynamic reality. This is realized at "the very time of their being formed," hence the identity of time and being, a key concept for Dōgen: "[Time is being(s), being(s) is all time]. . . . Mountains are time and seas are time. If they were not time, there would be no mountains and seas" (*SBGZ Uji*, p. 56.)

31. The Buddha-nature is not apart from the actual, everyday things around us.

you do not understand, that *totally dependent* is "whole dependence," is a depending whole."[32]

Samadhi and the six supernatural powers[33] are being revealed by means of the Buddha-nature. You should know that both the manifestation and non-manifestation of samadhi are totally dependent on the Buddha-nature. All six supernatural powers—whether they are being revealed by the Buddha-nature or not—are equally, totally dependent on the Buddha-nature.[34] The six supernatural powers are not simply those taught in the Agama sutras.[35] "Six" is the six supernatural powers perfected—"Three, three, before; three, three, after."[36] So do not investigate the six supernatural powers as "the clear bright tips of the myriad grasses are the clear bright purpose of the Buddha-patriarchs."[37] To do that would make you remain and become involved inextricably in the six super-

---

32. Each and every thing is wholly and utterly dependent on (cannot exist without) Buddha-nature. Given that the nondualistic activity of "depending" and the nondualistic function of "forming" are both the Buddha-nature, "wholeness" and "dependence" are absolutely reciprocal. On the one hand, this is to be understood, but on the other hand, even without our understanding, it is always being disclosed here at this very moment.

33. Six supernatural powers (*roku jinzū*). See p. 4, footnote 7.

34. Buddha-nature and supernatural powers, and samadhi, are inseparable, so the powers are dependent on the Buddha-nature, whether or not they are being revealed through the Buddha-nature.

35. Since samadhi and supernatural powers are themselves the Buddha-nature, they are not superhuman acts but the common activities of everyday life. Hence, they are different from the extraordinary faculties (eyes that see everywhere, ears that hear everything, etc.) enumerated in the Agama sutras of the Hinayana tradition.

36. An allusion from Case 35 of the *Pi-yen lu*. Wen-shu asked Wu-chu, "Where have you come from?" "The south," replied Chu. "What's Buddhism like in the south?" asked Shu. Chu said, "Monks of the latter-day Dharma do nothing but observe the precepts." Shu said, "How many are there?" "Three hundred, maybe five hundred," said Chu. Wu-chu asked Wen-shu, "How is Buddhism in these parts?" "Enlightened and unenlightened living together. Dragons and snakes mixed in together," Shu said. Chu said, "Many or few?" Shu said, "Three three before, three three after."

"Three three" is not an ordinary enumeration but indicates each individual entity immediately and distinctly manifested prior to mental discrimination. Here the phrase "six supernatural powers perfected" seems to indicate the clear and unmistakable manifestation (perfectly visible, perfectly audible, etc.) of each individual thing, that is, the manifestation of entire being as Buddha-nature.

37. This sentence refers to a saying of the T'ang layman P'ang Yün. P'ang told his daughter Ling-chao, "A man of old said that the clear, bright tips of the myriad grasses are the clear, bright purpose of Buddhas and patriarchs. How do you understand that?" Ling-chao repeated the same words (*LTHY*, ch. 6).

Each and every thing (the tips of myriad grasses), clearly and brightly distinguished in their suchness, reveals the true meaning of the Buddhas and patriarchs. Although profound, this statement is not free of conceptualization. Dōgen says that the clear, bright tips of grasses are the clear, bright tips of grasses, and this very fact is the Buddha-nature. Thus there is no need to penetrate the six supernatural powers by equating the clear tips of grasses to the purpose of the Buddhas.

natural powers. Nevertheless, that interference only occurs within the universal flow inside of the Buddha-nature Sea.[38]

*The Fifth Patriarch, Zen master Ta-man,[39] hailed from Huang-mei in Ch'i-chou. He was born without a father, and he attained the Way while still a child. [In his previous existence] he was a man named Tsai-sung Tao-che [The Pine-planting man of the Way]. In his old age, planting pine saplings at Hsi-shan in Ch'i-chou, he encountered the Fourth Zen Patriarch Tai-i, who was on an excursion away from the monastery. The Fourth Patriarch said, "I would like to transmit my Dharma to you, but I'm afraid you are too old. If you happen to get reborn into the human world, I will be waiting for you!" Tsai-sung nodded his agreement. Later, at the house of a man named Chou, he got reborn as the son of Chou's daughter. She abandoned the infant in a muddy creek, but he was protected by divine messengers. Seeing that he remained unharmed even after seven days had passed, the daughter retrieved him and raised him, and he passed a normal childhood. One day at the age of seven, he was travelling to Mount Huang-mei. He met the Fourth Patriarch Tai-i.[40] Even though he was still a child, Tai-i discerned that he possessed a physiognomy that set him apart from ordinary children.*

*The patriarch asked him, "What is your name?"*

*The boy replied, "I have a name, but it is not an ordinary name."*

*"What name is that?" asked the patriarch.*

*"It is Buddha-nature," said the boy.*

*"You have no Buddha-nature," said the patriarch.*

*"You say no [Buddha-nature] because Buddha-nature is emptiness," the boy replied.*

*The patriarch knew then that the boy was a vessel for the Buddha Dharma. He made him his attendant and, in the course of time, he imparted to him the treasure of the right Dharma Eye. Taking up residence on the eastern peak of Mount Huang-mei, the Fifth Patriarch spread the Dharma widely and exalted its profound depths.[41]*

When we penetrate the utterances of the two patriarchs, we find that the Fourth Patriarch's *What is your name?* contains a meaning of essential significance. In the past, there was a man from the land of "What."[42] There was a

---

38. When the student "investigates" (*sankyū* 参究) the six supernatural powers as the clear, bright tips of myriad grasses are the clear, bright tips of myriad grasses (not as the clear purpose of the Buddhas), that is, investigates them as themselves and not as Buddha-nature, they remain, and are inseparably taken up, in the supernatural powers (everyday life), an activity that is not apart from the Buddha-nature Sea.

39. Ta-man, the posthumous title of the Fifth Chinese Zen Patriarch Hung-jen, 602–675.

40. Tai-i, the posthumous title of the Fourth Patriarch Tao-hsin, 580–651.

41. The source for this passage has not been found.

42. "Someone asked, 'Master, what is you name?' 'My name is What,' he replied. 'What country are you from?' he asked. 'I'm a man of What country,' he answered" (*CTL*, ch. 27). Throughout

family named "What." Here, the Fourth Patriarch is teaching the boy: "Your family (name) is 'What.'" This is the same as saying "I am thus. You are thus too."[43]

The Fifth Patriarch said, *I have a name (nature),*[44] *but it is not an ordinary name.* In other words, a name (nature) that is self-identical with being[45] is not an ordinary name (nature), for an ordinary name (nature) is not self-identical with being.

When the Fourth Patriarch said, *What name is that?* "what" is an affirmation—he is "what-ing" an affirmation.[46] "What" is his name (nature). "What-ing" is possible, because it is affirmation: his affirmation is possible by virtue of "what." His name (nature) is both "it" (affirmation) and "what." It is infused in herbal tea. It is infused in your ordinary tea. It is your daily rice as well.[47]

The Fifth Patriarch said *It is Buddha-nature.*[48] Essentially, this means that "it" (affirmation) is the Buddha-nature. Because "it" is "what," "it" is the Buddha-nature.[49] But can "it" (affirmation) be fully comprehended only in "what" name? When affirmation is not affirmable, it is still the Buddha-nature.[50] Hence, although "it" (affirmation) is "what," is Buddha, when that is fully broken through and cast off, it is without fail a name (nature). Here, the name (nature) is "Chou" (All-pervading).[51] Yet this name (nature) is not received

---

this section Dōgen plays on the words "name" 姓 and "nature" 性, which are homophones in Sino-Japanese, with the question "What is your name" also signifying "What is your [true] nature?"

The word "What" 何 is being used as an interrogative—"What is it?"—and also in the sense of "What it is," signifying the nature or quiddity of the matter in question. We do not clarify something simply by asking "What is it," yet its very nature ("What it is") is at that moment appearing before us as it is in its true suchness. That is its original nature, or Buddha-nature, which is beyond the grasp of the intellect. Hence, "What" is Buddha-nature, undefinable, infinite, immeasurable.

43. These two sentences appear in the dialogue between Hui-neng and Nan-yüeh quoted above in footnote 5.

44. *I have a name (nature)* 姓即有. Against this normal reading, Dōgen reads word by word: "Name is being."

45. Being is Buddha-nature, in the sense of entire being-Buddha nature. See footnote 8.

46. Dōgen reads the sentence *What name is that?* (是何姓) word for word to mean: "Affirmation-what-name (nature)," with each of the three terms being identical. "What" is identical to "it" (as a Zen term the character *ze* 是 signifies affirmation). The inexpressible, nonobjectifiable "What," present right here, is itself "It," the self-affirmation (What-ing) of each being. This is its name, its (Buddha) nature.

47. Eating, drinking, and all of our everyday acts are our nature, our affirmation, nonobjectifiable expressions of universal reality (our "What-ing").

48. *It is Buddha-nature.* Word for word, the original here— 是佛性 —is closer to Dōgen's emphasis of "Affirmation is Buddha-nature" than the English translation conveys.

49. Affirmation is Buddha-nature because it is "What."

50. "It" (是), that is, affirmation, is not fully exhausted by "What" or "What-ing," nor is it solely affirmation either, for it is at the same time "not-It," not-affirmation, and that is the true Buddha-nature.

51. The Fifth Patriarch's family name was Chou 周, a word whose literal sense signifies

from your father, or from your ancestors; it has no resemblance to your mother's name and can of course never be compared with any other person's name.

The Fourth Patriarch said, *You have no Buddha-nature.*[52] This utterance reveals that although you are not someone else, you are entirely you, you are mu-Buddha-nature.[53] You should know, and you should study: What is the temporal occasion now, when you are mu-Buddha-nature? Are you mu-Buddha-nature when you have fully attained Buddhahood? Are you mu-Buddha-nature when you go beyond Buddhahood? Do not restrict mu-Buddha-nature by groping around for it.[54] At times, you practice and realize that mu-Buddha-nature is a single time of samadhi.[55] You should be asking and should be articulating: Am I mu-Buddha-nature when Buddha-nature attains Buddhahood? Am I mu-Buddha-nature when Buddha-nature begins aspiring for enlightenment? You should have even the temple pillars asking.[56] You should be asking the temple pillars. You should have the Buddha-nature asking too.

Hence, the utterance *mu-Buddha-nature* reverberates far beyond the chambers of the Fourth Patriarch. It was seen and heard in Huang-mei. It circulated freely in Chao-chou. It was exalted in Ta-kuei.[57] You must devote yourself without fail to the truth of *mu-Buddha-nature*. Never cease in your efforts. Although with *mu-Buddha-nature* you may have to grope your way along, there is a touchstone—What. There is a temporal condition—You. There is entrance

"wholeness," "all-pervading." Throughout this dialogue, Dōgen plays on this, as well as on the homophones *name* and *nature* (see footnote 42). Hence, the name Chou also refers to the patriarch's (Buddha) nature, which is all-pervading (entire being-Buddha-nature).

52. *You have no Buddha-nature* is the normal translation of the Chinese characters 無佛性 *mu-busshō*. Dōgen reads them, "You *are* mu-Buddha-nature" to underscore that Buddha-nature is prior to our discriminations and the dichotomy of having or not having Buddha-nature. Dōgen's idea of *mu-Buddha-nature* is not in opposition to "having Buddha-nature" (*u-busshō* 有佛性); it does not indicate the absence of "Buddha-nature." It is mu-Buddha-nature in its absolute sense, which is free from both "Buddha-nature" and "no-Buddha-nature." Dōgen is concerned with the Buddha-nature itself, which is nonsubstantial. To reflect this emphasis, throughout the following passages the term *mu-busshō* is translated "mu-Buddha-nature."

53. Here, "you" indicates not a particular person but *entire being*. Hence, inasmuch as you (the Fifth Patriarch) are "completely entrusted" with entire being, whether you call it Buddha-nature or something else, you are still mu-Buddha-nature.

54. The reality of mu-Buddha-nature is all-pervading. Do not try to restrict it or search for it with your discriminations.

55. *A single time of samadhi* 一時の三昧: samadhi taking place at each and every occasion or stage of time.

56. Cf. A monk asked, "What is the meaning of the First Patriarch's coming from the West?" Master Shih-t'ou answered, "Ask the temple pillar." "I don't understand," replied the monk. "I don't understand either," said the master (*Wu-teng hui-yüan,* ch. 29).

57. Huang-mei is another name for Hung-jen, the Fifth Patriarch, whose utterance of *mu-Buddha-nature* appears in the next section. Quotations by Chao-chou and Kuei-shan (Ta-kuei) also appear in later sections of *SBGZ Busshō.*

into its dynamic functioning—affirmation. There is a common name (nature)—Chou (All-pervading).[58] It is a direct and an immediate access.

The Fifth Patriarch's utterance *You say mu [Buddha-nature] because Buddha-nature is emptiness* articulates clearly and distinctly the truth that emptiness is not "no." In uttering *Buddha-nature-emptiness* one does not say "half a pound." One does not say "eight ounces." One says "mu." Because it is emptiness, you do not say emptiness. Because it is mu, you do not say mu. You say mu because it is Buddha-nature-emptiness.[59]

Hence every piece of mu is a touchstone to articulate emptiness; emptiness is the capacity to articulate mu. This is not the emptiness of "form is emptiness." "Form is emptiness" does not mean form is forced into emptiness, nor is it making form out of emptiness. It has to be the emptiness of "emptiness is emptiness." The emptiness of "emptiness is emptiness"[60] is a piece of rock in emptiness.[61] This being so, the Fourth and Fifth Patriarchs are asking and articulating Buddha-nature-mu, Buddha-nature-emptiness, and Buddha-nature-being.

*When the Sixth Chinese Patriarch Ch'an master Ta-chien[62] of Mount Ts'ao-hsi went to practice under the Fifth Patriarch of Mount Huang-mei for the first time, the Fifth Patriarch asked him, "Where do you come from?" He answered, "I am a man of Ling-nan."[63] The Fifth Patriarch said, "What have you come for?" "I've*

---

58 Here we follow the Ejō manuscript text and read 同生. Ōkubo has 同姓.

59. Buddha-nature is true emptiness, which is not mere nothingness but self-identical to the whole universe. Here Dōgen interprets the statement translated *Buddha-nature is emptiness* (佛性空) as "Buddha-nature-emptiness." As it is Buddha-nature-emptiness, it can only be expressed by saying "no," although emptiness itself is not no. If we say it is "half a pound," or "eight ounces," or anything else, we objectify and limit absolute emptiness, which is originally unbounded and unobjectifiable. By the same token, even though it is true emptiness or nothingness, we cannot speak of it using the words emptiness, or no, or nothingness. The key statement is, *He says "mu" because it is Buddha-nature-emptiness.* The various expressions using the word mu such as mu-Buddha-nature are merely touchstones used to articulate emptiness. Emptiness is the very power that articulates these expressions of mu.

60. *Form is emptiness, emptiness is form*, well-known lines from the *Heart Sutra*. "Form is emptiness" may suggest that there are two separate things, form and emptiness, and that they are identical. Dōgen stresses that emptiness, completely nonrelative and including all things, is dynamically and nondualistically form (*a piece of rock in emptiness*)—that is, it is "emptiness is absolutely emptiness," which is at once "form is absolutely form."

61. A monk asked Shih-shuang, "What is the meaning of Bodhidharma's coming from the west?" The master replied, "A rock in emptiness." The monk made a bow. The master said, "Do you understand?" "No," the monk replied. "A good thing you don't," said the master, "I'd break your skull if you did" (*CTL*, ch. 15).

62. Ta-chien Ch'an-shih, the posthumous title of Hui-neng, 638-713, the Sixth Zen Patriarch. This dialogue appears in *CTL*, ch. 3.

63. Ling-nan 嶺南, a remote region south of the Nan-ling mountain range dividing central and southern China, whose inhabitants were regarded as backward and uncultured.

*come to become a Buddha," he replied. The Fifth Patriarch said, "People of Ling-nan
have no Buddha-nature. How can you expect to attain Buddhahood?"*

This utterance does not mean that people of Ling-nan have no Buddha-
nature. Neither does it mean that they do have a Buddha-nature. It means,
"man of Ling-nan, you are mu-Buddha-nature."[64] *How can you expect to attain
Buddhahood?* means "What Buddha do you expect to attain?"[65]

Few in the past have clearly grasped the Buddha-nature's fundamental
principle. It is not something that can be understood by followers of the lesser
vehicles or by scholars of sutras and commentaries. It is solely transmitted person to person by descendants of the Buddhas and patriarchs.

A fundamental principle of the Buddha-nature[66] is that it is not invested
prior to attaining Buddhahood but incorporated upon attainment of Buddhahood. Buddha-nature and attainment of Buddhahood are always simultaneous.
This truth should be penetrated deeply in concentrated practice. There must
be twenty or even thirty years of diligent effort. It is not clarified even in the
higher stages of Bodhisattvahood.[67] It is the fundamental truth that articulates
"sentient beings are Buddha-nature," "sentient beings are mu-Buddha-nature."
The proper way is to study it as a Dharma incorporated upon the attainment of
Buddhahood.

If your study is not like this, it cannot be called the Buddha Dharma. If the
Buddha Dharma had not been studied like this, it would never have continued

---

64. Again Dōgen bends the Chinese, giving priority to religious meaning over normal grammatical syntax, reading the passage "Man of Ling-nan, you *are* (instead of *have*) no-[mu-] Buddha-
nature" to indicate this person from Ling-nan present before me is manifesting the Buddha-nature,
beyond any sense of "having" or "not having." It is sufficient to recognize his presence as such
without relating him to a principle such as Buddha-nature. The idea of "mu-Buddha-nature" is the
theme of the next ten paragraphs.

65. In keeping with his reading of the previous passage emphasizing Hui-neng as an immediate
manifestation of Buddha-nature, Dōgen interprets the question "How could you attain
Buddhahood?" (which at face value would be rhetorical, suggesting the impossibility of his attaining Buddha-nature) in a positive sense: there is no need to attain Buddha-nature, because it is
already attained.

66. This crucial passage refutes the notion of an inherent Buddha-nature as a conceptualization
that would divorce it from religious commitment and attainment. Dōgen stresses the dynamic
oneness of Buddha-nature and attainment that is manifested at the moment of enlightenment.
This also implies rejection of the idea that Buddha-nature is not inherent and is actualized only
through attainment, which would make it merely an objective goal. The words "manifesting simultaneously" (*dōsan* 同参) stress the manifestation of Buddha-nature at the moment of realization.

67. *The higher stages of Bodhisattvahood* translates the term *jisshō sangen* 十聖三賢, literally "ten
classes of sage" and "three groups of wise men." Mahayana Buddhism enumerates fifty-two stages
of discipline that Bodhisattvas practice on the way to final enlightenment. These stages are divided into five groups of ten steps each, with the final two steps belonging to supreme
enlightenment. The ten classes of sages are those practicing stages forty-one through fifty; the
three groups of wise men are those in stages 11 through 40.

to the present day. Unless you clarify this truth, the attainment of Buddha will be unclear to you, and you will never experience it. That is why when the Fifth Patriarch spoke to teach the Sixth Patriarch, he said, "Man of Ling-nan, you are mu-Buddha-nature." From the time you first encounter a Buddha and hear the Dharma, what is exceedingly difficult to understand and truly grasp is "all sentient beings are mu-Buddha-nature." Whether it comes from a good Buddhist teacher or from the sutras, that which cannot help giving joy when heard is "all sentient beings are mu-Buddha-nature." Unless your total experience is overflowing with "all sentient beings are mu-Buddha-nature," you have not experienced Buddha-nature. When the Sixth Patriarch sought with all his effort to attain Buddhahood and the Fifth Patriarch brought it about in him, there were then no other utterances, no other skillful means. All he did was to say, man of Ling-nan, you are mu-Buddha-nature.

You should know that the very uttering and hearing of mu-Buddha-nature was the direct and immediate path to Buddhahood. Because it was, he was a Buddha right at the very instant of mu-Buddha-nature. Not to have experienced or articulated mu-Buddha-nature is not to have attained Buddhahood.

The Sixth Patriarch said, people may have souths and norths, Buddha-nature does not.[68] You should take this utterance and concentrate deeply on penetrating its inner meaning. You must scrutinize these words about south and north directly, with mind unbared, for it is an utterance of fundamental significance. It contains an area of understanding that implies: although a person attains Buddhahood, Buddha-nature does not. I wonder if the Sixth Patriarch was aware of this implication.[69]

Buddhas such as Kashyapa and Shakyamuni inherited the capacity that the Fourth and Fifth Patriarchs' utterances mu-Buddha-nature have to totally restrict [ordinary understanding of the Buddha-nature].[70] They thus had the capacity when they attained Buddhahood and preached the Dharma to articu-

---

68. People may have souths and norths, Buddha-nature does not. In CTL these words follow the previous block quotation. Ordinarily they would signify that while people from the south may be different culturally from those in the north, there is no difference with regard to the Buddha-nature. Dōgen interprets the statement to make it adhere to the principle embodied in "What is this that thus comes"—the actual time and presence of Hui-neng himself, in which a southerner, prior to distinctions of south or north, is just a southerner and is as such the Buddha-nature.

69. As Buddha-nature is originally no different from Buddha-attainment, there is no way one could become the other. Dōgen asks if Hui-neng, when he said "Buddha-nature does not [have souths or norths]," was aware that Buddha-nature is Buddha-attainment and Buddha-attainment is Buddha-nature.

70. Their expression of mu-Buddha-nature keeps people from fixing on a false, objective understanding, which would try to grasp Buddha-nature as being this or that. Cf. "The moment I said it was 'this,' I'd miss the mark completely."

late the utterance "entire being-Buddha-nature."[71] How then could the being of *entire being* not succeed to the nothingness of absolute nothingness?

Hence, the words "mu-Buddha-nature" reverberate far beyond the chambers of the Fourth and Fifth Patriarchs. Had the Sixth Patriarch been a true man at this time, he would have concentrated all his effort on these words *mu-Buddha-nature*. He should have set aside the nothingness of being and nothingness and just asked himself, what is this Buddha-nature? He should have sought to discover what sort of thing the Buddha-nature is. People of today are no different. When they hear the words "Buddha-nature" they never question what it is. They seem concerned only with discussing the meaning of whether it exists or does not exist. A thoughtless and ill-considered occupation. The nothingness of all the various nothingnesses must study the nothingness of *mu-Buddha-nature*.[72]

As for the Sixth Patriarch's utterance, "People have norths and souths, Buddha-nature does not," it is something you should dip deep within again and again for a long period of time. You must have the capacity to take it in. You must quietly ponder the utterance in all of its facets. To imagine as the foolish do that the Sixth Patriarch has said, "Since human beings have substance, they have a south and north; but since the Buddha-nature is an all-pervading emptiness, devoid of substance, we cannot talk of its having a south or north"— that is unmitigated stupidity. You must cast that mistaken notion aside and apply yourself assiduously without a moment's delay.

*The Sixth Patriarch taught his disciple Hsing-ch'ang, "Impermanence is in itself the Buddha-nature. Permanence is, as such, the [dualistic] mind that discriminates all dharmas, good and bad."*[73]

The "impermanence" the Sixth Patriarch speaks of is not the impermanence deduced by the non-Buddhists and those of the Lesser Vehicle. Their patriarchs and those who have succeeded them preach impermanence, but they do not plumb its full extent.

---

71. The capacity of Kashyapa, Shakyamuni, and other Buddhas to utter "entire being-Buddha-nature" is grounded in the Fourth and Fifth Patriarchs' capacity to articulate "mu-Buddha nature." Since Shakyamuni lived prior to the Fourth and Fifth Patriarchs and Kashyapa Buddha prior to Shakyamuni, this is not possible in a chronological sense; Dōgen means that the realization of mu-Buddha nature explicitly articulated by the Fourth and Fifth Patriarchs was implicit in Shakyamuni's utterance *entire being-Buddha-nature*, because the realization of mu-Buddha-nature is always inherent in Buddhist practice.

72. The nothingness of mu-Buddha-nature is the fundamental source of all possible negations, so to attain their true meaning mu-Buddha-nature must return to nothing.

73. The episode in which these two sentences appear is translated in full in the appendix at the end of chapter 6, pp. 97–98.

The preaching, practicing, and realizing of impermanence by the impermanent themselves can be no other than impermanent. Those who are now manifesting themselves to save others are manifesting themselves [in their impermanence and preaching Dharma[74]—and *this* is the Buddha-nature.[75] Moreover, at times they manifest a long Dharma-body, and at times a short Dharma-body.[76]

The "permanent" saint is impermanent. The "permanent" unenlightened person is impermanent. For saints and ignorant people to be permanently saints or permanently ignorant would not be the Buddha-nature.[77] It would be only the foolish notions of small minds, restricted knowledge spun from discriminatory speculation. "Buddha" would thus be reduced to a small, limited body and "nature" to narrow, restricted activity. Hence, the Sixth Patriarch uttered the words *Impermanence is in itself the Buddha-nature*.[78] "Permanence" is prior to turning [into enlightenment. But] even though the Buddha-nature turns into the wisdom that cuts away the passions, or becomes the worldly passions being cut away, "prior to turning" is never associated with traces of coming or going. Hence, it is said to be permanent [in the sense of Buddha-nature as impermanence].[79]

For that reason, the very impermanence of grass and tree, thicket and

---

74. Here Dōgen modifies lines from the *Lotus Sutra* (*Universal Gate chapter*) describing transformations the Bodhisattva Kannon assumes in order to aid sentient beings.

75. The impermanence that Hui-neng speaks of defies any conceptual approach and can only be grasped by becoming one with it. Since he himself is impermanent, his preaching of impermanence is impermanence preaching itself, and all is thus totally impermanent.

76. Long things and short things are the Dharma-body just as they are. Cf. "Question: 'What is the long Dharma-body?' Answer: 'The staff is six feet long.' Question: 'What is the short Dharma-body?' Answer: 'The divining block is three inches short'" (*P'u teng lu*, ch. 2).

77. To suppose that the distinction between the saint and ordinary person is permanent is contrary to the true principle of the Buddha-nature, in which you realize that impermanence is the Buddha-nature, and thus that the condition of the saint or the unenlightened can change.

78. The Buddhist teaching that Buddha-nature is permanent and changeless (exemplified in the words of the *Nirvana Sutra*: "Constantly abiding is the Buddha-nature; generation and extinction is all dharmas") may give rise to a dogmatic understanding of Buddha-nature as fixed and immutable, transcending the changing world. Dōgen says that it is neither immutable being nor empty nonbeing and is not found apart from the impermanence of the world. It is realized at every point of time in the unceasing process of becoming—from being to nonbeing, nonbeing to being. It is this ceaseless process that Dōgen, with Hui-neng, indicates by "impermanence is Buddha-nature." Cf. "To understand when you hear [Buddha-]nature that water cannot flow and trees do not flourish and fade is not Buddhist. Shakyamuni Buddha said, 'Form, as it is, is [Buddha-]nature as it is'; thus flowers blossoming, leaves falling are, as such, [Buddha-] nature as it is. Yet the foolish think that in the realm of the Dharma-nature there can be no flowers opening or leaves falling'" (*SBGZ Hosshō*).

79. A difficult crux. We follow the syntactical order of the *Ōkubo* text, which at least offers a consistent reading of the text: "Permanence" in a fixed sense ("permanent" saint, etc.) represents an understanding prior to "turning into" enlightenment (awakening to Buddha-nature). The Buddha-

forest is the Buddha-nature. The very impermanence of people and things, body and mind is the Buddha-nature. Lands and nations, mountains and rivers are impermanent because they are Buddha-nature. Supreme, complete enlightenment, because it is the Buddha-nature, is impermanent. Great nirvana, because it is impermanent, is the Buddha-nature. Those holding the narrow views of the Lesser Vehicle, Buddhist scholars of the sutras and shastras, and the like will be suspicious, surprised, and frightened when confronted by these words of the Sixth Patriarch. If so, then they belong with the devils and heretics.

*The sage Ryūju Sonja, the Fourteenth Patriarch, is called Nagarjuna in Sanskrit;*[80] *in Chinese, he is called Lung-shu, Lung-sheng, and also Lung-meng. He was a native of western India. He went to southern India, where many believed that good fortune was obtainable through worldly acts, and preached the wondrous Dharma. Those who heard it said to one another, "Good fortune is the greatest thing you can receive in this world. This teacher speaks emptily of a 'Buddha-nature.' Who has ever seen it?"*

*Nagarjuna said, "If you want to see the Buddha-nature, first you must eliminate self-egoism."*[81]

*"How big is this Buddha-nature of yours?" they asked.*

*Nagarjuna said, "Buddha-nature is neither large nor small, broad nor narrow. It is not happiness or good fortune. It is not obtained as a reward for something. It is undying and unborn."*

*When the people understood the superlative nature of the truth embodied in Nagarjuna's teaching, all of them abandoned their original beliefs and became his followers.*

*At another time, as Nagarjuna was sitting, he manifested a body of absolute freedom—it was just like the round full moon. Not a person in the assembly saw the master's form. They heard only the sound of the Dharma.*

*Among the gathering was Kanadeva.*[82]

*"Can you discern his form?" he asked the others.*

*"Our eyes see nothing," they answered. "Our ears hear nothing. Our minds discern nothing. Our bodies experience nothing."*

---

nature itself, however, is free from all vestiges of its activity, even when it is manifested as *prajna*-wisdom, which severs the worldly passions obscuring the Buddha-nature. It is thus said to have "permanence," though only in the sense of "true permanence" (i.e., permanence that is at once impermanence).

80. This passage is found in *CTL*, ch. 1 (section on Nagarjuna). The Zen school regards Nagarjuna as the Fourteenth Patriarch in its Dharma lineage.

81. Self-egoism is a literal rendering of *ga-man* 我慢, a translation necessitated by the treatment Dōgen gives the word below.

82. Kanadeva, who lived in southern India in the third century, is fifteenth in the Zen school's patriarchal lineage.

*Kanadeva said, "That itself is the form of the sage Nagarjuna Sonja manifesting the Buddha-nature. He is doing it to teach us. How do I know this? Because the form of formless samadhi is like the full moon. The meaning of the Buddha-nature is absolutely empty, clear and distinct."*

*When Kanadeva finished speaking, the round shape disappeared, and Nagarjuna was sitting on his seat as before. He recited a verse:*

> Body manifesting a round moon shape,
> Expressing thereby the body of the Buddhas;
> Expounding Dharma, without any form,
> Expounding without sight or sound.

You should know true expounding is not directly manifested in sound or sight; true Dharma preaching has no form. Nagarjuna preached the Buddha-nature widely in countless sermons. Here I present only a brief account of one small portion of them.

*If you want to see the Buddha-nature, you must first eliminate self-egoism.*[83] You must without fail discern and affirm the essential significance of this. It does not mean the absence of seeing. Seeing is in itself the elimination of self-egoism. The self is not a single self. Self-egoism exists in great variety. Eliminating is of great diversity. But, nevertheless, all are seeing Buddha-nature. You must accustom yourself to your own ordinary seeing.

Do not associate an utterance such as *It is neither large nor small* with the commonplaces voiced by the unenlightened or by those of the Lesser Vehicle. To conceive distortedly of the Buddha-nature merely as a vast immensity is a case of illusory discrimination. You should think, in just the same way that you hear, the truth that is totally tied up in the utterance *It is neither large nor small* being made right here and now. That is because you are using hearing that is no different from thinking.

Now let us attend to the verse Nagarjuna uttered. It says *Body manifesting a round moon shape, Expressing thereby the body of the Buddhas.*[84] Because the manifesting body is, as such, *expressing thereby* all Buddha-bodies, it is the shape

---

83. Dōgen interprets this sentence so as to reject dualistic implications in the words "see the Buddha-nature" and "eliminate self-egoism," and to emphasize that Buddha-nature is not something "seen" after self-egoism is eliminated; it is manifesting itself directly even in the act of "eliminating." Dōgen's reading of these words is analogous to his reading of the *Nirvana Sutra* passage quoted earlier: "If you wish to know the Buddha-nature's meaning, you must contemplate temporal conditions."

84. A literal interpretation of the first two lines of Nagarjuna's verse: *Body manifesting a round moon shape, Expressing thereby the body of the Buddhas*, which suggests somewhat dualistically that the round moon shape is a temporarily manifested Transformation-body of the Buddha, and that the body of the Buddhas and Nagarjuna's body are not originally one, is rejected by Dōgen, who wishes to emphasize that Nagarjuna's actual body itself is the body of the Buddhas (hence mani-

of the round moon. Hence, all sizes—longs and shorts—and all forms—round and square—are to be studied in his manifesting body. To be unaware of [the nondualistic relation of] *body* and *manifesting* is not only to be ignorant of the shape of the round moon; it is not the body of Buddhas either. The ignorant think, "He is temporarily manifesting a Transformation body—that is what is meant by *a round moon shape*." But that is an illusory notion, held by those who have not received authentic transmission of the Buddha Way. Where, and when, could you manifest another body not your own?

You should know without any doubt that at that very time Nagarjuna was just sitting there on the high seat. The form in which he manifested his body was no different from the form of any one of us sitting here right now. Right now our own bodies are manifesting a round moon shape.

The "manifesting body" is not square or round, is not existing or nonexisting, is not revealed or concealed, is not a compound of 84,000 *skandhas*—it is just a body manifesting itself.

As for the *round moon shape*, "Where do you think you are, speaking of the fineness or roughness of the moon?"[85]

Since self and ego are from the first excluded from this *manifested body*, the manifesting body is not Nagarjuna; it is the body of all Buddhas. Since it is *expressing thereby*, it breaks through beyond all Buddha-bodies. Because of that, it is completely free of Buddhahood. Although clearly and distinctly embodying the form of the full moon/Buddha-nature, it is not a round moon shape set out on display. Much less is there any sight or sound in the preaching it expounds. The manifesting body is not form or mind. It is not a *skandha*, base, or field.[86]

---

festing a round and perfect moonlike shape). Therefore, this round moon shape is not the tempo-rary manifestation of a Transformation-body (*Nirmāṇa-kāya*) and is neither round, square, fine, rough, revealed, or concealed. In an attempt to show the nondualistic relation between the body actually being manifested and the Buddha-body, Dōgen reads the Japanese expression *motte hyōsu* (or *motte arawasu*: 以て表（わ）す) "to express [something] by means of . . . ," which has dualistic undertones, as the single Chinese term *ihyō* 以表, translated here as "expressing thereby [all Bud-dha bodies]."

85. This statement derives from the following episode. Zen master Huang-po made obeisance before a statue of the Buddha. The clerk of the monastery approached and said, "We are told not to seek it in Buddha, in Dharma, or in Sangha. Why are you bowing, master?" Huang-po immediately slapped him in the face. "I'm not seeking it in Buddha, in Dharma, or in Sangha. I'm just bowing as I always do." Then he gave the clerk another slap. The clerk said, "You're too rough." "Where do you think you are, prattling about 'rough' and 'fine'?" said Huang-po, and he gave him another slap. Dōgen comments on this dialogue in *SBGZ Gyōji*.

86. *Skandha*, base, or field 蘊處界. The five *skandhas* or constituent elements of all existences (*goun* 五蘊): form, perception, conception, volition, consciousness. The *twelve bases* or sense fields (*jūnisho* 十二處): the six sense organs (eyes, ears, nose, tongue, body, and mind) and the objective fields of sight, sound, smell, taste, touch, and thought. The *eighteen fields* 十八界 are the *twelve bases* and the corresponding *six discernments* that take place in sense perception. Taken together, they represent the whole world, including man himself, as the field of sense perception.

Although it is identical to *skandha*, base, and field, it is *expressing thereby*, and it is the original body of all Buddhas. This is a *skandha* preaching the Dharma. It has no established form, and when an unestablished form is formless samadhi as well, it is the *manifesting body*.

The assembly is now looking at the full moon shape and yet *their eyes see nothing*. That is due to the dynamic working of the Dharma-preaching *skandha*, to the no-sight, no-sound of the absolutely free body being manifested. Now concealed, now revealed—it is only a backward step or forward step of the same round shape. At the very time *Nagarjuna was sitting manifesting a body of absolute freedom, not a person in the assembly saw the master's form. They heard only the sound of the Dharma.*

Kanadeva, the legitimate successor to Nagarjuna, clearly discerned the full moon shape. He knew the perfect round moon shape, knew the body manifesting, knew all Buddha-natures, knew all Buddha-bodies. Even though many entered Nagarjuna's inner chambers and received his truth in the same way that water is transferred from one vessel to another, none of them could bear comparison with Kanadeva, the spiritual leader of the assembly, the man worthy to share his master's Dharma seat and fully qualified to occupy it by himself. He rightly transmitted the supreme, great Dharma, the treasure of the right Dharma eye, just as did Mahakashyapa, who occupied the foremost seat at Vulture Peak.

Before Nagarjuna converted to the Buddha Way, when he followed a non-Buddhist teaching, his disciples were numerous. Upon entering the Buddha Way, however, he gave them all their leave. After he became a Buddha-patriarch, it was to Kanadeva alone, the legitimate heir to receive and pass on his Dharma, that he rightly transmitted the treasure of the great Dharma eye. This was the personal, one-to-one transmission of the supreme Buddha Way.

In spite of this, dissembling, would-be teachers have frequently come forth, claiming, "We too are rightful Dharma heirs of the great teacher Nagarjuna." They have written treatises and put together commentaries and passed them off as Nagarjuna's. But they were not written by Nagarjuna. These men whom Nagarjuna had formerly disavowed have thus deluded and confused men and devas alike. Disciples of Buddha should have no doubts on this point: unless a work has been transmitted by Kanadeva, it is not an utterance of Nagarjuna. This knowledge is in itself attainment of right faith. Yet there are many who have accepted and transmitted these writings fully aware that they are spurious. We must pity and deplore the stupidity and ignorance of sentient beings who would thus defame the *prajna* wisdom of the Buddhas.

At that time, the sage Kanadeva pointed to Nagarjuna's manifesting body and declared to the assembly, *That itself is the form of the sage Nagarjuna Sonja manifesting the Buddha-nature. He is doing it to teach us. How do I know this?*

*Because the form of formless samadhi is like the full moon. The meaning of the Buddha-nature is absolutely empty, clear, and distinct.*

Now what bag of skin past or present who has seen or heard the Buddha Dharma that at present extends throughout the realms of devas, humans, and all of the trichiliocosmic universe has uttered, "The form of his body manifesting is the Buddha-nature"? Kanadeva alone, among all of those in the great billion-world universe, has made such an utterance. Others say only that the Buddha-nature is not seen with the eye, heard with the ear, discerned with the mind, and so forth. They have not said that the manifesting body is the Buddha-nature, because they did not know it. It is not because the patriarchal teachers begrudged them that knowledge. They could not see or hear it because their eyes and ears were obstructed. As their bodies had not yet experienced it, it was not possible for them to discern it. When gazing and bowing reverently before the full-moon form of formless samadhi, their eyes did not see it. That is to say, *the meaning of the Buddha-nature is absolutely empty, clear and distinct.*

The manifesting body preaching the Buddha-nature is therefore clear and distinct—and it is absolute emptiness. The preaching Buddha-nature bodily manifesting itself is *thereby expressing* the original body of all Buddhas. Nowhere is there even one Buddha not making this *thereby expressing* his Buddha-body. The Buddha-body is a manifesting body, and it is the Buddha-nature manifesting the body. Even Buddhas' and patriarchs' capacity to utter and understand that the four great elements and five *skandhas* [are the Buddha-nature][87] is a momentary expression of the manifesting body. Once you speak of the Buddha-body, it is *skandhas*, bases, and fields, just as they are, manifesting the Buddha-body. All merits of whatever kind are in fact this very same merit. The merit of Buddhahood is the all-pervading, all-encompassing activity of this manifesting. The comings and goings of all of these infinite, boundless merits are a single moment of this manifesting body.

After the master Nagarjuna and the disciple Kanadeva, there have been many down through the ages in the three countries (India, China, Japan) who have studied the Buddha Dharma, but there has never been anyone who could make the utterances they did. How many sutra-teachers, how many scholars of the shastras, have strayed from the path of these Buddha-patriarchs?

For a long time people in the land of the Sung have endeavored to illustrate this episode in painting, but they have never been able to paint it in their bodies, paint it in their minds, paint it in the sky, or paint it on walls. In vain attempts to paint it with a brush tip, they have made depictions of a round,

---

87. Cf. A monk asked, "I've heard you say that when the world perishes, its nature will not. What is that nature?" Chao-chou said, "Four elements, five *skandhas*." The monk said, "That's what perishes. What about its nature?" Chao-chou said. "Four elements, five *skandhas*" (*LTHY*, ch. 6).

mirrorlike circle on the Dharma seat, and made it out to be the moon-round shape of Nagarjuna's manifesting body. In the hundreds of years that have come and gone since then, these depictions have been like gold dust in the eyes, blinding people, yet no one has pointed out the error. How sad that matters have been allowed to go unremedied like this! If you understand that the round moon shape manifested by the body is an all-round shape, it is no more than a painted rice cake. It would be ludicrous in the extreme to divert yourself by playing with that.

How sad to think that not a single layperson or priest throughout the land of the Sung has ever heard or understood Nagarjuna's words, has ever regarded or become familiar with Kanadeva's words; much less has anyone truly been in agreement with the manifesting body. They are blind to the round moon, and they throw the full moon into eclipse. This comes from neglecting to "search out the ancient ways," from insufficient "yearning for the past."[88] Old Buddhas! New Buddhas! Encounter the real manifesting body! Do not waste your time admiring a painted rice cake!

You must know that in painting the form of the body manifesting a round moon shape, the form of the manifesting body must be there on the Dharma seat. Eyebrows must be directly and authentically raised, eyes directly and authentically blinked. Skin, flesh, bone, and marrow, the treasure of the right Dharma eye, must without fail be sitting immovably in zazen. This transmits Mahakashyapa's smile, for it is becoming a Buddha, becoming a patriarch. If this picture is not a moon-shape, the shape of suchness is not there; it does not preach the Dharma; it makes no sight, no sound, no sermon. If you would seek the manifesting body, you must trace the shape of the round moon. When you trace the shape of the round moon, you can trace only the shape of the round moon, because the manifesting body is the round-moon shape. When you want to paint the round-moon shape, you must trace the shape of the full moon, you must manifest the full-moon shape.

Nevertheless, not to paint the manifesting body, not to paint the round moon, not to paint the full-moon shape, not to trace the body of Buddhas, not to be *thereby expressing*, not to trace the preaching Dharma, and to trace in vain a picture of a rice cake—what possibly can come of that?

Set your eyes on it, right now, quickly! Who right at this moment cannot eat his fill and satisfy his hunger?

The moon is a round form; the roundness is the body manifesting. When you study the roundness, do not study it as a round coin, do not regard it as a rice cake. The shape of the body is the body of the round moon. The form of

---

88. Two well-known expressions, the first from the opening words of the *Book of History*, the second from the *Latter Han History*.

suchness is the form of the full moon—a round coin, a round rice cake, must be studied in this roundness.[89]

My Zen pilgrimage took me to the land of the Sung where, in autumn of the sixteenth year of Chia-tung [1223],[90] I first visited the Kuang-li Zen temple on Mount A-yü-wang.[91] While I was there, I saw painted on the walls of the western corridor in the main hall transformed images of the thirty-three patriarchs of India and China.[92] At that time, I did not comprehend them. Later, in the first year of Pao-ch'ing [1225], during the summer retreat, I visited the temple again. As I was walking along the corridor with Ch'eng-kuei of Shu, guestmaster at the monastery,[93] I came before the image of Nagarjuna. I asked Ch'eng-kuei, "What transformation is depicted here?"

"That's Nagarjuna, bodily manifesting a moon-like shape," he answered.

But the noseholes in the face that uttered those words were drawing no breath; the words themselves were hollow in his mouth.

"Yes, indeed," I said, "just like a picture of a rice cake, isn't it?"

He laughed loudly. But there was no edge to his laugh. It could not have even penetrated a painted rice cake.

While we proceeded to the Relic Hall and to the six famous sights of the monastery, I brought the subject up several more times, but Ch'eng-kuei showed no sign that he had any doubts about it. Several other monks ventured opinions as well, but their comments too were totally off the mark.

"Let's ask the head priest about it," I said. The head priest at that time was Ta-kuang.[94]

---

89. The round, moonlike shape is not Nagarjuna manifesting himself in that particular form as a Transformation-body in order to teach sentient beings; it is his actual body being manifested, which is, as such, the original body of all Buddhas. The roundness of the moon is formless, beyond any particular shape. We must not study the moon's roundness in some round object, like, say, a coin; rather, we must study such objects in the formless roundness of the moon.

90. In the third month of 1223, at age twenty-four, Dōgen left the port of Hakata in Kyushu; he arrived at the port of Ming-chou at the end of the fourth month. He reached Mount T'ien-t'ung in the seventh month, then left and made a pilgrimage to masters in other monasteries. The episode he relates here presumably took place during this pilgrimage.

91. Mount A-yü-wang (in present Chekiang) was, with Mount T'ien-t'ung, one of the "Five Mountains" of contemporary Chinese Zen.

92. *Transformed images* 變相 *hensō*. *Hensō* refer to paintings or drawings, instructive in purpose, illustrating episodes from Buddhist scripture and tradition; depictions of the circumstances of the Pure Land, Hell, and so on. The pictures of the thirty-three Zen patriarchs referred to here were presumably based on episodes found in Zen texts. Nagarjuna was apparently painted as a round, moonlike shape.

93. Ch'eng-kuei of Shu 西蜀の成桂, n.d.

94. Ta-kuang 大光. Little else is known of this priest. He is mentioned in the *Hōkyō-ki* (section 20), the practice diary Dōgen kept during his study in China. In reply to Dōgen's question about a teaching he heard from Ta-kuang at Mount A-yü-wang (which Dōgen said he was doubtful about), Ju-ching remarked that Ta-kuang and all other Zen masters of the day were "irresponsible."

"He has no noseholes," replied Ch'eng-kuei.[95] "He couldn't give you an answer. What could you learn from him?"

So I did not ask Ta-kuang after all, and Brother Kuei himself, despite the way he spoke, did not understand either. None of the monks who heard our discussion were able to venture any utterance. Past generations of head priests at Mount A-yü-wang[96] who have gazed at this picture must not have harbored any doubts about it, for they had not changed it.

Things that are undepictable are best left unpainted. If they must be painted at all, they can only be painted straight to the point. Yet the body manifesting the shape of the round moon has never yet been painted.

Because they have not awakened from the mistaken view that the Buddha-nature is identical to their present perceptions and discriminations, they are depriving themselves of a gateway through which to penetrate either the words "Buddha-nature" or the words "mu-Buddha-nature." Those who are even being taught that they must make some utterance are few and far between. You should know that this state of neglect stems from a corruption that is almost beyond hope of recovery. Everywhere you go there are head priests who pass their entire lifetimes without once uttering the words "Buddha-nature." Some of them say, "A person who only listens to the Dharma teaching may talk about the Buddha-nature, but not a monk who is engaged in Zen practice." Such people are no different from the beasts. A pack of devils who have strayed into our Way of the Buddha-tathagatas and defile it! Is there only "listening to the Dharma teaching" in the Buddha Way? Is there only "engaging in Zen practice" in the Buddha Way? You must realize that in the Buddha Way [distinctions between] listening to the Buddhist teaching and practicing Zen have never existed.

*National Teacher Ch'i-an of Hang-chou, in Yen-kuan hsien, a distinguished priest and disciple of Ma-tsu, once taught his disciples, "All sentient beings have the Buddha-nature."*[97]

---

95. *He has no noseholes*: he lacked true religious attainment that would enable him to function freely.

96. Previous head priests at the A-yü-wang monastery included such famous figures as Ta-hui Tsung-kao, 1089–1163, and Cho-an Te-kuang, 1121–1203.

97. This quotation and the next are found in *LTHY*, ch. 7. "Ta-kuei (posthumous name of Kuei-shan Ling-yü, 771–853) used to teach his assembly of monks that sentient beings have no Buddha-nature. So when Yen-kuan [another name for National Teacher Ch'i-an] told his assembly that 'all sentient beings have the Buddha-nature,' two monks in his brotherhood made a special trip to Ta-kuei's temple to sound the matter out. But after listening to Ta-kuei, they still failed to appreciate his true capacity, and this caused them to have feelings of disrespect toward the master. One day as they were sitting in the garden of Ta-kuei's temple, they saw Ta-kuei's disciple Yang-shan coming and called out, 'Brother! We must all devote ourselves to the practice of the Buddha Dharma. It is not an easy thing.' Yang-shan proceeded to inscribe a circle in the air with his finger. He made a motion of holding it out toward them, then he cast it behind him. Then, spreading out

The words "all sentient beings" should be penetrated forthwith. The inner and external karma of sentient beings is not the same.[98] Their ways of viewing things are different. There are unenlightened, non-Buddhist adherents of the three vehicles, five vehicles, and so forth.[99] As for "all sentient beings," in the Buddha Way all things possessed of mind are called sentient beings, because mind is, as such, sentient being. Things not possessed of mind are also sentient beings, because sentient beings are, as such, mind. Hence, all mind is sentient being, and sentient beings all are being Buddha-nature.[100] Grass and tree, nation and state are mind. Because they are mind, they are sentient being.[101] Because they are sentient being, they are being Buddha-nature. Sun, moon, stars, and planets are mind. Because they are mind, they are sentient being. Because they are sentient being, they are being Buddha-nature. The "being Buddha-nature" uttered by National Teacher Ch'i-an is just like this. If it were not like this, it would not be the "being Buddha-nature" that is uttered in the Buddha Way.

Here the essential significance of the National Teacher's utterance is simply: "All sentient beings being Buddha-nature." In that case, they could not be "being Buddha-nature" unless they were sentient beings. So we should ask the National Teacher: "Are all Buddhas being Buddha-nature, or not?" We should probe and question things in this way. We should examine why it is not said "all sentient beings are as such Buddha-nature," why, instead, it is said "all sentient beings are being Buddha-nature." The "being" of being Buddha-nature must without fail fall away. This "falling away" is a single steel rod. "A single steel rod" is the path of a bird in flight. Hence, "all Buddha-natures are being

---

his arms, he posed some questions to them, but they didn't know how to respond. Yang-shan counselled them, 'We must all devote ourselves to the practice of the Buddha's Dharma. It is not an easy thing. Farewell.' The two monks set out to return to Yen-kuan's temple, but after travelling about thirty *li*, one of them had an abrupt realization. Sighing deeply, he said, 'I should have known Ta-kuei's "Sentient beings have no Buddha-nature" was not mistaken.' He returned to Ta-kuei's temple, leaving the other monk to continue on; but he too, after proceeding several more *li*, as he was crossing a stream, experienced a realization. He sighed to himself, 'It's perfectly obvious he should say such a thing,' and then he also returned to Ta-kuei."

98. *Inner and external karma* refers to two aspects of karmic retribution: *shō-hō* 正報 or direct retribution (e.g., human life attained as a result of past karma) and *e-hō* 依報, various ancillary circumstances in one's environment on which one's life is dependent.

99. The *three vehicles* are the three forms of teaching peculiar to the shravakas, pratyeka-buddhas, and bodhisattvas, respectively. Humans and devas are added to make the *five vehicles*.

100. Dōgen reads Ch'i-an's words quoted at the head of this section—*All sentient beings have the Buddha-nature*—to mean *All sentient beings are being Buddha-nature*.

101. Here *mind* is synonymous with Buddha-nature. Cf. Dōgen's adaptation of well-known words from the *Avatamsaka Sutra*: "Throughout the three worlds all is mind. Apart from this mind there is no dharma. Mind, Buddha, sentient beings—these three are not different" (*SBGZ Sangai-yuishin*). Since for Dōgen all being is sentient being, the term *sentient beings* includes things not usually considered possessed of mind.

sentient being." This is a truth that not only preaches away sentient beings but also preaches completely away Buddha-nature as well.[102]

Even if the National Teacher did not give direct expression to his understanding just as it was, that does not mean there will not come a time when he will be able to do so. Nor does it mean the words he speaks at this time are ineffectual or devoid of essential meaning. Again, although he himself has not necessarily grasped the truth he embodies in himself, he is nonetheless possessed of the four elements, five *skandhas*, and skin, flesh, bone, and marrow body [of the Buddha-nature]. Sometimes, in this way, a real utterance may take a lifetime to make. Sometimes, one may be engaged for several lifetimes in making an utterance [without knowing it].

*Ch'an master Ta-yüan of Mount Ta-kuei once said to the assembly of monks: "All sentient beings have no Buddha-nature."*[103]

Among those who heard him in the human world and in the deva realms were some beings of outstanding capacity, who rejoiced in it. Those thrown into wondering doubt by it were not unknown either. Shakyamuni expounded "all sentient beings without exception have the Buddha-nature." Ta-kuei expounded "all sentient beings have no Buddha-nature." The words "have" and "do not have" are totally different in principle. It is understandable that doubts should arise as to which utterance is correct. But in the Buddha Way, "all sentient beings have no Buddha-nature" is alone preeminent. With his words "have the Buddha-nature" Yen-kuan seems to be putting out a hand in concert with the old Buddha Shakyamuni: nonetheless, it cannot help being a case of two men holding up one staff.[104] Now Ta-kuei is different. In his case, "one staff swallows up both men."[105] Of course, National Teacher Yen-kuan was a child of Ma-tsu. Ta-kuei was Ma-tsu's grandchild. Yet in the way of his Dharma grandfather, Dharma grandson Ta-kuei proves to be an old graybeard, and in the way of his Dharma father, the Dharma son Yen-kuan is still a callow youth.[106]

---

102. Here Dōgen emphasizes the "falling away" (*datsuraku* 脱落) of the being included in the idea of "being Buddha-nature"; this falling away itself is awakening, a clearly coherent reality that is still as free and traceless as the flight of birds. A *single steel rod* (*ichijō tetsu* 一條鉄) is a metaphor suggesting the ceaseless, coherent, and unchangeable reality working throughout the process of phenomenal change. *Path of a bird in flight* (*chōdō* 鳥道) refers to totally unfettered activity in which no aftertraces are left. Cf. *Tung-shan lu*: "Addressing an assembly of monks, Tung-shan said, 'I have three ways. The way of birds. The way of mysteriousness. The extending of my hand.'"

103. *LTHY*, ch. 7, where this quotation continues from the previous one (see footnote 97).

104. That is, there is no difference between Yen-kuan's "have the Buddha-nature" and Shakyamuni's.

105. His utterance of "no Buddha-nature" swallows up (usurps or appropriates completely) the utterances of Shakyamuni and Yen-kuan.

106. Yen-kuan Ch'i-an was a disciple of Ma-tsu Tao-i. Kuei-shan Ling-yü was an heir of Ma-tsu's student Po-chang Huai-hai. Cf. above, footnote 97.

The principle at work in Ta-kuei's words is the principle of "all sentient beings have no Buddha-nature." That does not mean that Ta-kuei's "no Buddha-nature" is boundless and lacks definition, for it is present right there, received and maintained in the scriptures he embodies within his own house.[107] It should be probed further: How could all sentient beings be Buddha-nature? How could they have a Buddha-nature? If a sentient being had a Buddha-nature, he would belong with the devil-heretics. It would be ushering in a devil and trying to set him on top of a sentient being. Since Buddha-nature is just Buddha-nature, sentient beings are just sentient beings. It is not that sentient beings are from the first endowed with the Buddha-nature.

Here the essential point is even though you seek the Buddha-nature hoping to endow yourself with it, Buddha-nature is not something to appear now for the first time. Do not imagine it is a matter of "Chang drinking and Li getting drunk."[108] If sentient beings originally possessed the Buddha-nature, they would not be sentient beings. Since they are sentient beings, they are not the Buddha-nature at all.

That is why Po-chang said, "*To preach that sentient beings have the Buddha-nature is to disparage Buddha, Dharma, and Sangha. To preach that sentient beings have no Buddha-nature is also to disparage Buddha, Dharma, and Sangha.*"[109]

Therefore, whether it is "have Buddha-nature" or "have no Buddha-nature," both end up by disparaging the Three Treasures. But regardless of the disparagement, you cannot get by without making an utterance. Now let me ask Ta-kuei and Po-chang, "It may well be disparagement, but has the Buddha-nature been really preached or not?

---

107. Reading Ta-kuei's words "all sentient beings are no Buddha-nature," Dōgen stresses that they are a vital truth that Ta-kuei has made his own, not a mere negation without any coherent criterion.

108. Sentient beings are not originally endowed with Buddha-nature (which would render practice unnecessary), nor is Buddha-nature achieved by practice. Buddha-nature and sentient beings are not separate, so it is not a case of Chang's Buddha-nature drinking and Li's sentient being getting drunk. Cf. "A monk asked, 'Will there be a Buddha Dharma in the new year?' 'No,' said the master. The monk said, 'Every day is a good day. Every year is a good year. Why do you say No?' The master said, 'Mr. Chang drinks, Mr. Li gets drunk'" (*LTHY*, ch. 26).

109. This quotation appears in the *T'ien-sheng kuang-teng lu*, ch. 9. The rest of the passage goes: "Speak of having the Buddha-nature and you disparage the Dharma by attaching to it. Preach the existence of the Buddha-nature and you disparage it with needless amplification. Preach the nonexistence of the Buddha-nature and you disparage it by reducing it. Say it is both existent and nonexistent and you create a discrepancy. Say it is neither existent nor nonexistent and you disparage it with frivolous utterance. Endeavor from the first to say nothing and sentient beings will never reach deliverance. Endeavor to preach it from the first and sentient beings will attach to your words, and that will give rise to speculation about it. Whatever the case, the benefit is small, the harm great. Hence, Shakyamuni said, 'I would rather enter nirvana directly, and not preach the Dharma at all.'" Despite these admonitions, Dōgen says below, "We cannot go without making an utterance."

Even granting it has been preached, wouldn't the Buddha-nature be totally implicated in the preaching? Any preaching of it would have to occur together with the hearing of it. Moreover, I must ask Ta-kuei, "Even though you articulated that all sentient beings have no Buddha-nature, you did not say all Buddha-natures have no sentient being, or that all Buddha-natures have no Buddha-nature. Still less could you have seen, even in your dreams, that all Buddhas have no Buddha-nature. Now let's see if you can come up with a response!"

Ch'an master Ta-chih of Mount Po-chang addressed the assembly.[110] "Buddha is the highest vehicle, the highest of all wisdoms, the person who maintains the Buddha Way. It is Buddha being Buddha-nature. It is a guiding teacher. It is being able to utilize a Way that is utterly unhindered. It is unimpeded wisdom. In all this, it readily utilizes cause and effect. It is the free activity of seeking enlightenment and enlightening others. It is the vehicle that carries on cause and effect. Negotiating life, it is not held back by life. Negotiating death, it is not hindered by death. Negotiating the five skandhas, it is like a gate freely opening. It suffers no restriction by the five skandhas. It goes and stops at will, leaves and enters unhindered. Inasmuch as it is thus, distinctions between high and low, intelligent and ignorant, are immaterial. And since this is the same even down to the body of the tiniest ant, all is a wondrous land of purity beyond our comprehension.[111]

Such are Po-chang's words. "Five skandhas" is this present, indestructible body of ours.[112] Our present activity moment-to-moment, a gate freely opening, does not suffer impediments from the five skandhas. Completely utilizing life, it cannot be held back by life. Completely utilizing death, it cannot be obstructed by death. Do not vainly cherish life. Do not foolishly dread death.[113] They are where the Buddha-nature is. Clinging with attachment to life, shrinking in abhorrence from death, is unBuddhist. To realize that life and death are a combination of conditions manifesting themselves before your eyes is to be able to utilize a Way that is totally unhindered. This is the Buddha of the highest vehicle. Where this Buddha is, there is the wondrous Land of Purity.

Huang-po was sitting in Nan-ch'üan's tea room. Nan-ch'üan said, "'Practicing dhyana and prajna equally, you clearly see the Buddha-nature.'[114] What is the essence

---

110. Ta-chih is Po-chang's posthumous title.

111. This passage is found in T'ien-sheng kuang-teng lu, ch. 9.

112. See footnote 106 above.

113. See SBGZ Shōji, p. 106.

114. This statement by Nan-ch'üan is from the Nirvana Sutra: "Bodhisattvas of the ten stages, because they have great power from prajna-wisdom but little from samadhi, cannot see Buddha-nature clearly. Shravakas and pratyeka Buddhas, because they have great power from samadhi but little from prajna-wisdom, cannot see the Buddha-nature. Buddhas, World-honored Ones, because they possess dhyana and prajna in equal measure, clearly see Buddha-nature, see it clear and unobstructed, like a fruit in the palm of their hand."

*of that teaching?" Huang-po said, "The essence is attained when you are not depend-
ing on a single thing throughout the twenty-four hours." Nan-ch'üan said, "Elder
monk, isn't that the attainment you yourself have achieved?" Huang-po said: "No,
not at all." Nan-ch'üan said, "Forget for now about the cost of the food and drink
you've had here—who's going to pay for those straw sandals of yours?" With that,
Huang-po abandoned the conversation.*[115]

The essential meaning of *practicing dhyana and prajna equally* is not: since
the practice of *dhyana* does not impinge on the practice of *prajna*, you clearly
see the Buddha-nature when both are practiced equally. Rather, it is clearly
seeing the Buddha-nature is a practice in which *dhyana* and *prajna* are in equal
balance. Nan-ch'üan is articulating, "*What* is the meaning of *That*."[116] He is in
effect saying that clearly seeing the Buddha-nature is the act of 'Who'." To say
"If you practice Buddha and nature equally, you will clearly see the Buddha-
nature. What is the meaning of That," is also an authentic utterance of truth.

*Huang-po said, When you are not depending on a single thing throughout the
twenty-four hours.* Essentially, this means even though the twenty-four hours
exist within the twenty-four hours of each day, they are nondepending. Because
not depending on a single thing is within the twenty-four hours, it is the
Buddha-nature clearly seeing.[117] As for the twenty-four hours, when is not the
time of their arrival? In what land does their arrival not occur? Are the twenty-
four hours referred to here twenty-four hours in the human world? Are they
twenty-four hours somewhere else? Or is this the temporary arrival of twenty-
four hours in a Land of White Silver?[118] Whatever the case, whether it is our
own world or another world, it is nondepending. In fact, this lies within the
twenty-four hours and can only be nondepending.

*Elder monk, isn't that the attainment you yourself have achieved?* is the same
as saying, "Isn't that the Buddha-nature clearly seeing?" Even though Nan-
ch'üan makes this utterance about it being Huang-po's attainment, Huang-po
must not turn his head, as if it referred to him. Although it may apply very well
to Huang-po, it does not refer to Huang-po. Huang-po certainly is not necessarily only himself, because a master's way of attainment is utterly unrestricted
and all-pervading.

---

115. This is found in the *T'ien-sheng kuang-teng lu*, ch. 8. Huang-po Hsi-yün and Nan-ch'üan
P'u-yüan were both disciples of Po-chang. The "tea room" is the room the abbot used for receiving
guests.

116. See above, footnote 46.

117. When you are totally free at all times and not depending on anything, Buddha-nature
manifests itself; rather, this nondepending itself is Buddha-nature. Cf. Lin-chi's "Buddhas are born
from non-depending. Awaken to non-depending, and there is no Buddha to be obtained" (*The
Record of Lin-chi*, trans. Ruth Sasaki, p. 14).

118. A name given to the Buddha-land of the Bodhisattva Samantabhadra.

Huang-po said, *No, not at all.*[119] In Sung China, when a person is asked about some talent or ability he may possess, even if he wishes to acknowledge the ability, he answers, "No, not at all." Hence, the words "No, not at all" do not literally mean, "No, not at all. They are not to be taken at face value. As for the mode of understanding of a Zen master, even though he is a master, or even though he is a Huang-po, when he speaks he has no choice but to say, "No, not at all." When a water buffalo appears, it can only say *"Ohng, Ohng."* This kind of utterance is authentic. Try to utter the essential meaning of his utterance! Make an utterance on his utterance!

*Nan-ch'üan said, Forget for now about the cost of the food and drink you've had here—who's going to pay for those straw sandals of yours?* You should commit yourself for many lifetimes to probing the meaning of this utterance. You should concentrate your mind and study deliberately why it is he does not concern himself with the cost of the food and drink. The reason he is so concerned about the straw sandals is because he assumes that in the years of pilgrimage many pairs of them must have been worn out. Here, one must say: "If I couldn't pay for the sandals, I wouldn't put them on to begin with." Again, one must say, "Oh, two or three pairs." It has to be utterances like those. It has to have that kind of essential significance.

*With that, Huang-po abandoned the conversation.* This means that he cut the conversation off, but it was not because he did not accept Nan-ch'üan's response. With priests of the true stamp, that could never occur. You have to realize that the words in their silence are the same as the razor edge on a laugh. It is the Buddha-nature clearly seeing—rice gruel and rice in inexhaustible abundance.

*Kuei-shan brought this episode up with Yang-shan. He said: "Nan-ch'üan was too slippery for Huang-po, wasn't he?" "Not at all," said Yang-shan. "You must understand that Huang-po has a capacity that subdues tigers." "There's such mastery in the way you see things," said Kuei-shan.*[120]

What Kuei-shan means is: Huang-po could not trap Nan-ch'üan that time, could he?

*Yang-shan said, Huang-po has a capacity that subdues tigers. Once he has caught one, he scratches it behind the ears.*[121]

---

119. "No, not at all" (*fukan* 不敢). The original term signifies a certain reticence on the part of the speaker. "I shouldn't say so myself, but yes, it is so." The translation is closer to the letter, preserving the negative mode, because of Dōgen's treatment of this response in his commentary.

120. From *T'ien-sheng kuang-teng lu*, ch. 8, where it follows immediately upon the previous quotation. Kuei-shan Ling-yü was an heir of Huang-po. Yang-shan Hui-chi was a disciple of Kuei-shan. Above, page 86, Kuei-shan is referred to as Ta-kuei.

121. In his comments on Yang-shan's "Huang-po has a capacity that subdues tigers" Dōgen refers to two aspects of the Buddha-nature's activity: catching tigers, or attaining enlightenment,

*Catching a tiger, scratching it behind the ears; going among different
    creatures;
Clearly seeing Buddha-nature, opening the Eye.
Buddha-nature clearly seeing, losing the Eye.
Hurry ! Quickly ! Say something!*

Buddha-nature sees things with great mastery. Hence, for a thing or even
half a thing, there is never any depending. A hundred things, a thousand things,
all are undepending. A hundred times, a thousand times, all are undepending.
That is why it is said:

> One [universal] wicker trap, at all hours,
> Depending, non-depending, like vines on a tree.
> Throughout heaven, over all heaven,
> After that, no words remain.[122]

*A monk asked Chao-chou Chen-chi Ta-shih, "Does that dog have the Buddha-nature,
or not?"*[123] The meaning of this question must be clarified. It asks neither
whether a dog has the Buddha-nature or whether it does not have the Buddha-
nature. It asks, "Does a man of iron still practice the Way?"[124] Chao-chou blun-

---

and scratching them behind the ears, utilizing enlightenment, or going beyond enlightenment. In
the verse, "Clearly seeing Buddha-nature" refers to the first aspect, hence, "opening the Eye." The
aspect of utilizing enlightenment without attachment is "Buddha-nature clearly seeing, losing the
Eye." Dōgen then exhorts students who understand this principle of the Buddha-nature to express
it in an utterance of their own.

122. Nothing in the universe is apart from the Buddha-nature, nor is it depending on any other
thing. Even a wicker trap (*rarō*: metaphor for the binding involvements of the evil passions) is a
manifestation of the universal Buddha-nature. The dependence of the unenlightened person and
the independence of the enlightened are both manifestations of the Buddha-nature, just as the
vines and creepers (*kattō*) clinging to trees and the trees being clinged to equally manifest the
original nature of vines and trees. The final lines, *Throughout heaven . . .* allude to Huang-po
stopping the conversation.

123. A monk asked Chao-chou, "Does that dog have the Buddha-nature or not?" Chao-chou
said, "Yes" (*u*). The monk said, "If so, why does the Buddha-nature push into such a lowly bag of
skin?" Chao-chou said, "Because it does it knowingly, deliberately transgressing." Another monk
asked, "Does that dog have the Buddha-nature or not?" Chao-chou said, "No" (*mu*). The monk
said, "All sentient beings without exception have the Buddha-nature. Why doesn't a dog have it?"
Chao-chou said, "Because it exists within karmic consciousness" (*Hung-chih sung-ku*, case 18). It
should be pointed out that the two characters *u* 有 and *mu* 無, which occur throughout this section,
have been translated in different ways according to the contexts in which they appear. For example,
*u* appears as "It has" in Chao-chou's answer, and elsewhere as "being," "existence," and "exists."
*Mu* is given as *mu* and also sometimes translated as "No."

124. *A man of iron* (*tekkan* 鉄漢), one who has awakened to the Buddha-nature, his practice
accomplished. Not taking the monk's words (Does that dog have the Buddha-nature?) at face
value, Dōgen sees it as a penetrating question, pressing the master about the truth of the Buddha-
nature: whether an enlightened one (the Buddha-nature itself) must still engage in practice.

dered into a poison hand, and his resentment may be intense, but it is a means of "seeing half a real saint at last, after thirty years."[125]

*Chao-chou said, "No" (mu).*[126] Hearing this word, the course of practice to be pursued opens up. The mu the Buddha-nature declares itself to be, the mu the dog declares itself to be, both must be utterances like Chao-chou's mu. So does the mu a bystander calls out. Such a mu is a sun with stone-melting power.

*The monk said, "All sentient beings, every one, have the Buddha-nature. Why doesn't the dog?"* What this essentially says is: were there no sentient beings, there would be no Buddha-nature; there would be no dog either. Essentially, it means "What." Dog. Buddha-nature. What need have they to be called mu?[127]

*Chao-chou said, "It is because the dog exists in karmic consciousness."* The meaning of these words is that existence for the sake of others is karmic consciousness. Although his existence in karmic consciousness is existence for the sake of others, it is dog-mu, it is Buddha-nature-mu. Karmic consciousness never understands the dog. How could the dog encounter the Buddha-nature?[128] Whether we speak of existence in karmic consciousness, existence for the sake of others, or of dog-mu or Buddha-nature-mu, they are always karmic consciousness.[129]

*A monk asked Chao-chou, "Does that dog have the Buddha-nature, or not?"* This question signifies that the monk has skillfully gotten hold of Chao-chou. We thus see that making utterances and posing questions about the Buddha-nature are ordinary, rice-eating, tea-drinking occurrences in the lives of Buddhas and patriarchs.

*Chao-chou said, "It has."*

---

125. A *poison hand* (*dokushu* 毒手) refers apparently to the monk and the question he raises. There is an allusion to a story about Zen master Shih-kung, who always kept an arrow notched in his bow ready to shoot. When San-ping approached him, Shih-kung said, "Watch for the arrow!" San-ping threw his chest out. Shih-kung said, "For thirty years I've had an arrow notched in this bow. Today, finally, I succeeded in shooting half a saint" (*CTL*, ch. 14).

126. Chao-chou's answer "No" (*mu*) does not signify the opposite of "having." Like his other answer ("It has") to the same question, it is a direct, total manifestation of the Buddha-nature, beyond having or not having and embracing both.

127. Dōgen says that the point of the monk's question is What?-*qua*-Buddha-nature. As such, this is similar to "What is this that thus comes?" and "What" that came before. There is no need for Chao-chou even to call it mu.

128. Reaching beneath the face value of Chao-chou's words, Dōgen interprets "karmic consciousness" (*gosshiki*) as an assertion that there is no Buddha-nature apart from karmic consciousness. Karmic consciousness is, as such, the dog; the dog, as such, is the Buddha-nature. One cannot "understand" or "encounter" the other (cf. above, p. 63: "Within entire being it is impossible, even with the greatest swiftness, to encounter sentient beings").

129. In this sentence, there is a rhetorical contrast between *u* or "existence" and *mu* that is not reflected in the English.

The manner of this "has" is not the has employed by exegetes of the Doctrinal schools. It is not the "has" posited by the Sarvastivadin scholars.[130] You must go beyond them and learn the Buddha-being.[131] Buddha-being is Chao-chou's being. Chao-chou's being is the dog's being. The dog's being is Buddha-nature being.

The monk said, "If it already has the Buddha-nature, what's the use of its pushing into such a bag of skin?" This monk's utterance asks whether Chao-chou's being is present being, past being, or established being, and we would have to reply that the "original being"[132] in Chao-chou's utterance appears to refer to one being among various other beings. But in fact it is "original being," shining alone. Should original being be something that pushes into? Should it be something that does not push into? The act of pushing into this bag of skin is a case of "erroneous striving," but it is not therefore in vain.

Chao-chou said, It's because it does it knowingly—it deliberately transgresses." As a mundane utterance, these words have long circulated in the world. But now it is Chao-chou's utterance. He is saying that it transgresses on purpose, in full knowledge of what it does. There are probably few people who would not have doubts about this. The words "pushing into" are difficult to understand in this context,[133] but in fact they are not really needed here.[134] Not only that, "If you want to know the Undying Man in his hermitage, you must not leave your own bag of skin!"[135] The Undying Man, whoever he may be, is never at any time separated from his bag of skin. "To transgress knowingly" is not necessarily "pushing into such a bag of skin." "Pushing into such a bag of skin" is not

---

130. Sarvastivadin. One of the schools of Hinayana Buddhism, which held the view that all things really exist ("has" 有 also means "exist"). Its teachings were widely studied in China and Japan.

131. Buddha-being. Being that transcends conceptual, dualistic views of being.

132. Original being renders Dōgen's interpretive reading of the characters ki-u 既有, which in the previous italicized quotation are translated If it already has the Buddha-nature. Again, the difference between "having" and "being" (both the same character 有 in the original) is significant. For Dōgen "original being" is Buddha-nature as a complete manifestation of entire being. All-pervading and absolutely incomparable, it "shines alone" (komei 孤明).

133. Pushing into (dōnyū 撞入) presupposes the duality of something pushing in and someplace being pushed into. Since nothing is apart from the Buddha-nature, it is more correct to say that the pushing into itself is the Buddha-nature.

134. An allusion to the following story in LTHY, ch. 8. "Yang-shan asked Secretary Lu, 'I've heard you attained enlightenment while reading a sutra. Is that so?' Lu said, 'I attained that place of rest and joy as I was reading the Nirvana Sutra, where it says, "Enter nirvana without severing the evil passions."' Yang-shan held up his whisk and said, 'Just this. How could you enter here?' Lu said, 'I can't even use the word "enter."' Yang-shan said, 'The word "enter" has nothing to do with you.' Lu thereupon rose and left."

135. Lines from Shih-t'ou Hsi-ch'ien's Ts'ao-an ko (CTL, ch. 30). The Undying Man is the Buddha-nature, which is not apart from your own bag of skin (the human body).

necessarily "knowingly and deliberately transgressing." It has to be "deliberately transgressing," because it is "knowing." You should be aware that this "deliberately transgressing" may, as such, contain concealed within it daily activity that constitutes the emancipated body of suchness.[136] This is what is meant by "pushing into." At the very time the daily activity constituting the emancipated body of suchness is concealed within it, it is concealed from you and from others as well. But although that is indeed true, do not say you are not yet free of ignorance. You leader of donkeys! You horse-follower![137]

And that is not all. The eminent priest Yün-chu said, "You may learn all there is to know about the Buddha Dharma, but in doing so you completely falsify the bearing of your mind."[138] Hence, even if your partial, halfway study of the Buddha's Dharma has long been in error—for days or even months on end—it still cannot be anything but the dog pushing into such a bag of skin. It is a case of "knowingly transgressing," but that itself is no other than being Buddha-being.

*At an assembly of the practicers under Ch'ang-sha Ch'ing-ts'en, Minister Chu said, "An earthworm is cut into two parts. The two parts move. In which part do you think the Buddha-nature is found?" The master said, "Have no illusions!" Chu said, "What about the movement?" The master said, "Just undispersed wind and fire."*[139]

Should the Minister's *An earthworm is cut into two parts* be explained as meaning it was one part before it was cut in two? No, in the house of the Buddhas and patriarchs, that could never be true. The earthworm was not originally one. It did not become two because it was cut. You should concentrate your effort directly, in practice, on what is being said here about one and two.

---

136. Read literally, the words "knowingly and deliberately transgressing" declare from a relative point of view that the Buddha-nature dares to push into (enter) a lowly creature like a dog. Dōgen, from a nonrelative position, asserts that "deliberately transgressing" is a function of the Buddha-nature. This activity thus contains concealed within it "the daily activity constituting the emancipated body of suchness."

137. "Master Chen Mu-chou asked a newly arrived monk where he came from. The monk just stared at him wide-eyed. The master said, 'You leader of donkeys! You horse-follower!'" (*CTL*, ch. 2).

138. Yün-chu Tao-ying, a disciple of Tung-shan Liang-chieh, co-founder of the Ts'ao-tung (Sōtō) school to which Dōgen belonged. Probably based on the version in *LTHY*, ch. 22.

139. This dialogue appears in *LTHY*, ch. 6. Minister Chu said to master Ch'ang-sha, "An earthworm is cut into two parts. The two parts move. In which part do you think the Buddha-nature is found?" Ch'ang-sha said, "Have no illusions!" The Minister said, "What about the movement?" Ch'ang-sha said, "You ought to know that it is wind and fire still undispersed." The Minister made no answer. Ch'ang-sha called out to him. He responded. Ch'ang-sha said, "Isn't that your real life?" The Minister said, "There can't be another true person apart from what responded just now." Ch'ang-sha said, "But I mustn't make you the reigning emperor." The Minister said, "In that case, I couldn't give you any response. Doesn't that make me a true person?" Ch'ang-sha said, "It isn't merely a matter of answering or not answering. This very thing has been the source of birth and death from infinite kalpas past." Then he made a verse: "Practicers of the Way fail to discern true reality / Just because they imagine it is their ordinary consciousness / Thus the root of birth and death for infinite kalpas past/ Is called by the ignorant the body of suchness."

Does the two parts of *the two parts move* mean that prior to the cutting there was one part? Or that one part transcends Buddhahood? The utterance *two parts* has nothing to do with whether or not the Minister understood it. Do not overlook what *the two parts move* has to say! Although the two parts that were cut were originally one thing, is there another "one thing" in addition to the original one thing? To say of their movement that *the two parts move* can only mean movement in the same sense that *dhyana* , which moves the passions, and *prajna*, which removes them, are both equally movement.[140]

*In which part do you think the Buddha-nature is found?* This should be: the Buddha-nature is cut into two parts. In which part do you think the earthworm is found? Now here is an utterance that must be penetrated with great care.

Does *The two parts move. In which part do you think the Buddha-nature is found?* mean if both move, they are not worthy to contain the Buddha-nature? Or does it mean they both move, so it is equally movement, but where in that is the Buddha-nature found?

*The master said, "Have no illusions!"* The essential meaning of this is What? Thus it means not having illusions. Therefore, you should penetrate, through practice, whether this means in the two parts both moving there is no illusory thought, or this movement is not illusory thinking. Or is it just in the Buddha-nature, there are no illusory thoughts. Or is he simply saying, without reference to the Buddha-nature or the two parts, "Have no illusions!"[141]

*What about the movement?* Does this mean since they are moving, does another Buddha-nature have to be added? Or does it try to express if they move it is not the Buddha-nature?

*Undispersed wind and fire*[142] brings the Buddha-nature into manifestation. Should we say that [the movement] is the Buddha-nature? Or should we say that it is wind and fire? We must not say that Buddha-nature and wind and fire appear together. We must not say that one appears, while the other does not. Nor can we say that wind and fire are in and of themselves the Buddha-nature. Therefore, Ch'ang-sha does not say there is a Buddha-nature in the earthworm, or that earthworms have no Buddha-nature. He just says *undispersed wind and*

---

140. This alludes to a passage in the *Nirvana Sutra* ("Lion's Roar" chapter): "It is like pulling up an obstinate tree. First you take hold of it and work it around, then it is easy to pull it up. *Prajna* and *dhyana* work in the same way. The passions are first broken loose by means of *dhyana*; they are then eliminated using *prajna*."

141. *Makumōzō* 莫妄想. As ordinarily understood, this typical Zen statement may suggest a dualistic viewpoint. Thus Dōgen reads it, "There is no illusion," or simply "No illusion!" to indicate the authentic state of human being.

142. *Undispersed wind and fire* (*fūka-misan* 風火未散). Normally this would refer to existence—represented by wind and fire, two of the four constituent elements of the material world—that has not yet perished, that is, the elements that have come together and constitute life and body have not yet dispersed. Dōgen interprets it to indicate the original state of things in suchness, prior to the "dispersal" into elements.

*fire*. The living actuality of the Buddha-nature must be construed from Ch'ang-sha's utterance.

You must quietly concentrate your efforts on the words *undispersed wind and fire*. What is the ruling principle of *undispersed*? Does *undispersed* refer to accumulations of wind and fire that have not yet reached the stage where they must disintegrate and scatter? It could hardly mean that. Wind and fire undispersed is the Buddha expounding the Dharma. Undispersed wind and fire is the Dharma expounding Buddha. That is to say, it is the arrival of the time of one sound preaching the Dharma. One sound preaching the Dharma is the arrival of the time. The Dharma is one sound, because it is the one-sound Dharma.[143]

Moreover, to think the Buddha-nature exists only for the duration of life and cannot exist in death betrays an extremely feeble understanding. The time of life is being Buddha-nature, no Buddha-nature. The time of death is being Buddha-nature, no Buddha-nature.

If there is a question about the "dispersal or nondispersal" of wind and fire, it can only be about the dispersal or nondispersal of the Buddha-nature. Even the time of dispersal must be Buddha-nature being, Buddha-nature mu. Even the time of nondispersal must be being Buddha-nature, no Buddha-nature. Hence, to cling to the mistaken view that the presence of the Buddha-nature depends on whether or not there is movement, that its spiritual working depends on whether or not there is consciousness, or that it is inherent or not in being perceived to be so—that is not Buddhism.

For infinite kalpas past, foolish people in great number have regarded the consciousness mind as the Buddha-nature. They have regarded it as the "original person"[144]—how laughably absurd! In making further utterances about the Buddha-nature—and this won't be a case of "entering the water and getting covered with mud"—the Buddha-nature is a fence, a wall, a tile, a pebble.[145] When making an utterance beyond this [you can only say] "What is this Buddha-nature?" Do you fully understand? Three heads! Eight arms![146]

---

143. Although the Buddha's preaching has a single sound and meaning, it is heard by sentient beings in various different ways. "The Buddha preaches the Dharma with a single sound, and sentient beings hear and understand it differently in their own ways" (*Vimalakirti Sutra*, "Buddha Lands" chapter). ˙

144. This is based on the verse Ch'ang-sha composed for Minister Chu. See above, footnote 139.

145. *Entering the water and getting covered with mud* is a Zen phrase used to describe the enlightened person's return to the world of defilement to help others. Dōgen says that he will not, in stating the Buddha-nature is a fence, wall, and so on, be guilty of explaining too much for students, since Buddha-nature is *entire being* and there is nothing apart from it. Cf. *SBGZ Hotsumujō-shin*: the National Teacher Ta-cheng said, "Fences, walls, tiles, pebbles—those are the minds of old Buddhas".

146. *Three Heads! Eight Arms!* An allusion to the ashura or "fighting demon," with perhaps a suggestion of a being inconceivable to ordinary rational thinking.

APPENDIX TO CHAPTER SIX

The monk Chih-ch'e was a native of Kiangsi. . . . After the Zen school split into southern and northern factions, though the leaders of the two groups made no such discriminations themselves, rivalry grew between their followers, which gave rise to intense feelings of partiality. Followers of the northern faction arbitrarily put forward their leader Shen-hsiu as the Sixth Patriarch and were thus envious when it became widely known that the patriarchal robe had been transmitted to Hui-neng, leader of the southern group. They enlisted the services of Hsing-ch'ang and told him to murder Hui-neng. Hui-neng, with his all-knowing mind, perceived what they were about. He placed ten taels of silver in his room. One dark night, Hsing-ch'ang entered the room and prepared to strike Hui-neng. Hui-neng stretched out his neck in readiness. Hsing-ch'ang struck three times but was unable to inflict any injury. Hui-neng said, "A just sword does not miss its mark; an unjust sword cannot strike true. I'll give you money, but not my life." Hsing-ch'ang fell over in a swoon. When he revived, he penitently begged Hui-neng to pity him and make him a monk. Handing him the money, Hui-neng said, "You had best leave. I'm afraid my followers might try to take revenge. In the future you can disguise yourself and come here again. I will receive you then." Hsing-ch'ang followed Hui-neng's advice and escaped into the night.

Afterward, he went to a priest and had himself ordained, receiving the full precepts and devoting himself to religious practice. One day, recalling Hui-neng's words, he traveled to visit him. Hui-neng said, "You've been on my mind all this time. What has kept you so long?" Hsing-ch'ang said, "Before, you forgave my criminal behavior. Today, I am engaged in austere discipline as a monk. But I have been unable to find any way to requite your kindness. I will just do all I can to transmit the Dharma for the sake of others. I always study the *Nirvana Sutra,* but I haven't been able to grasp the meaning of permanence and impermanence. Please, master, in your compassion, would you briefly explain it for me?" Hui-neng said, "Impermanence is the Buddha-nature. Permanence is the mind that discriminates all the various dharmas good and bad." "That's not at all what the sutra says," replied Hsing-ch'ang. "I transmit the seal of the Buddha-mind, why would I deliberately say something that is counter to the Buddha's sutras?" said Hui-neng. "The sutra preaches that the Buddha-nature is permanent, but you say it is impermanent. The sutra says all dharmas good and bad and even the mind of enlightenment are impermanent. You say they are permanent," said Hsing-ch'ang. "Those differences only deepen my doubt." Hui-neng said, "Once when I heard the nun Wu Chin-tsang read the

See chapter 6, p. 75, footnote 73.

*Nirvana Sutra*, I made some impromptu comments on it. Not one of my words or their meaning was in disagreement with the sutra's. It's the same when I teach you. I never say anything different from the sutra." Hsing-ch'ang said, "My powers of understanding are poor. Please, could you explain it in more detail?" Hui-neng said, "If the Buddha-nature were permanent, what would be the need to preach beyond that about all dharmas good and bad? Even in the passage of an entire kalpa, there would not be a single person who would ever raise the mind of enlightenment. That is why I preach impermanence, and that itself is the way of true permanence preached by the Buddha. If, on the other hand, all dharmas were impermanent, then each thing would have a selfhood and take part in birth-and-death, and there would be areas to which true permanence did not reach. Therefore, I preach permanence, and it is just the same as the meaning of true impermanence preached by the Buddha. The attachment to illusory permanence of unenlightened non-Buddhists, and the discriminations of followers of the two vehicles that take permanence as impermanence—which together make up the eight topsy-turvy views—were refuted as distorted, one-sided views by the Buddha when he expounded his complete and perfect teaching of nirvana and made explicit the teaching of true permanence, true pleasure, true self, and true purity. By relying merely on words, you now subvert their inner meaning. If you mistake the perfect and subtle words the Buddha spoke just prior to his demise as indicating nihilistic impermanence or lifeless permanence, you could get no benefit from the *Nirvana Sutra*, even though you read it a thousand times over. Hsing-ch'ang suddenly attained a great enlightenment. He made a verse:

> Holding firmly to the mind of impermanence
> The Buddha preached permanence;
> Those unaware of his skillful means
> Just seize on a pebble in a spring pool.
> Though I now put forth no effort at all,
> Buddha-nature is right under my nose.
> It is not received from my teacher,
> Nor is it something I gained either.

Hui-neng said, "You have penetrated it. I must give you the name Chih-ch'e (Aspiration Penetrates)." Chih-ch'e bowed in thanks and left (from the *Platform Sutra of the Sixth Patriarch* [*Liu-tsu t'an-ching*]).

# SEVEN

# Sammai-Ō-Zammai
# 三昧王三昧

## (THE KING OF SAMADHIS SAMADHI)

According to a colophon attached to *Sammai-Ō-Zammai*, it was delivered on the fifteenth day, the second month, the second year of Kangen [1244] at Kippō-shōja [Yoshimine-dera] in the province of Echizen. The words *Sammai-Ō-zammai* appear in Nagarjuna's *Ta chih tu lun:* "It is called the King of Samadhis Samadhi because all other samadhis of various kinds are included in it. It is like all the myriad rivers and rivulets of the human world flowing as tributaries into the great ocean; or like the fact that all people are vassals of the king of the realm." For Dōgen, it refers to zazen, the authentic practice for followers of Buddhism (*Ōkubo*, vol. 1, 539–42).

### SAMMAI-Ō-ZAMMAI

To sit crosslegged is to take a leap straightaway transcending the entire world and to find oneself within the exceedingly sublime quarters of the Buddhas and patriarchs.[1] To sit crosslegged is to trample over the heads of all the devil heretics and become the Person within the Buddhas' and patriarchs' innermost precincts. This Dharma and this alone is the way to transcend the highest

---

1. To sit crosslegged—*kekkafuza*—that is, the full lotus position.

reaches of the Buddhas and patriarchs. It is for this reason that Buddhas and patriarchs practice it and never exert their efforts elsewhere.

You should know that the total world of sitting is far different from all other total worlds.[2] In penetrating the true nature of this difference, you discern and affirm the arising of the religious mind, the practice, enlightenment, and nirvana of the Buddhas and patriarchs.[3]

At the very time of your sitting, you should examine exhaustively whether the total world is vertical or horizontal.[4] At that very time, what is the sitting itself? Is it wheeling about in perfect freedom? Is it like the spontaneous vigor of a leaping fish? Is it thinking? Or not thinking? Is it doing? Is it non-doing? Is it sitting within sitting? Is it sitting within body and mind? Or is it sitting that has cast off sitting within sitting, sitting within body and mind, and the like? You should examine exhaustively in this way thousands or tens of thousands of such details. It should be the body sitting crosslegged. It should be the mind sitting crosslegged. It should be body and mind cast off sitting crosslegged.

My late master, the old Buddha, said: "The practice of Zen (sanzen) is body and mind falling away.[5] It is attained only in single-minded sitting. There is no need for incense-offerings, homage-paying, nembutsu, penance disciplines, or sutra-readings."

In the past four or five hundred years it is my late master alone who plucked out the eye of the Buddhas and patriarchs and sat within its core.[6] There have been few in China who could compare to him. Rare are those who have understood that sitting is the Buddha Dharma, and the Buddha Dharma is sitting. Some may have known experientially that sitting is the Buddha Dharma, but none of them has known sitting as sitting. How, then, could any-

---

2. All other total worlds—that is, the total world of non-Buddhists and of those Buddhists who do not practice crosslegged sitting. The total, all-encompassing world of the zazen sitter is beyond them.

3. Discern and affirm . . . patriarchs. In the total world of zazen, you realize the truth that the arising of the religious mind (bodhichitta), practice, enlightenment, and nirvana are not relative states of a spiritual process, as is usually thought by those confined to "all other realms." Each of the four is absolute and includes the other three as well, a truth that is affirmed or confirmed in the sitter.

4. Vertical or horizontal—the commentary SBGZ monge has: "In crosslegged sitting . . . there is no vertical time division of past, present, future; horizontally, the world of all the ten directions disappears. All is cast off. 'Vertical' and 'horizontal' are provisional names; they have no real existence" (SBGZ chūkai zensho, v. 8).

5. The "old Buddha" is Dōgen's Chinese master Ju-ching. The words quoted here appear in the fifteenth section of Dōgen's practice journal Hōkyō-ki.

6. That is, since the time of the T'ang Zen master Po-chang, revered author of the earliest rules of Zen monasticism, which included a text on zazen.

one have been able to protect and uphold the Buddha Dharma as the Buddha
Dharma?

Hence, there is a mind sitting, and it is not the same as a body sitting.
There is a body sitting and it is not the same as a mind sitting. There is sitting
with body and mind cast off, and it is not the same as sitting with body and
mind cast off.[7] Once you attain this state of suchness and attain the harmoni-
ous unity of activity and understanding possessed by the Buddha-patriarchs,
you examine exhaustively all the thoughts and views of this attainment.

*Shakyamuni Buddha preached to the assembly of monks:*

> *If you are sitting crosslegged*
> *Body and mind realize samadhi*
> *Great virtue revered by all is yours*
> *You are like the sun illuminating the world.*
> *Lethargy, mind-numbing sloth are dispelled*
> *The body is light, the body is tireless*
> *Even awakening comes quickly and easily*
> *Sitting serenely like a dragon coiled.*
> *Faced with depictions of crosslegged sitting*
> *King Mara staggers with fright*
> *Must he not recoil in greater terror*
> *Seeing a Wayfarer seated calm and unmoved?*[8]

Even King Mara is amazed, distressed, and filled with fear when he sees picto-
rial depictions of crosslegged sitting.[9] Imagine the terror he feels when he is
faced with actual crosslegged sitting itself, the merit of which is impossible to
fully calculate. It then follows that wherever there is crosslegged sitting, there
also is bliss and virtue beyond measure. Why?

*Shakyamuni Buddha's next words to the assembly of monks were, "It is be-*
*cause of this that I sit crosslegged." He then instructed all his disciples to sit just like*
*this. Non-Buddhists seek the Way by constantly standing on tiptoe, by remaining*
*constantly standing, or by entwining their legs about their necks. The minds of these*
*overzealous practicers are sunk in a sea of falsehood. The configuration and postures*
*they assume are unstable. Hence the Buddha taught his followers to sit crosslegged in*
*upright posture. It is because with the body upright, the mind is easily rectified. In*

---

7. For a mind sitting there is nothing apart from mind, and thus it is different from a body
sitting. The same holds true for a body sitting. Although in a relative sense sitting with body and
mind cast off might be said to transcend the first two cases mentioned, as soon as that differentiation is made, it is no longer truly "sitting with body and mind cast off."

8. This verse appears in slightly different wording in the *Ta chih tu lun*, ch. 7.

9. King Mara: "The Destroyer" or Evil One, who obstructs the progress of the Buddhist practicer.

*upright sitting the mind does not grow slothful. With an upright mind and right thought, mental activity is concentrated right before you. If the mind strays, if the body starts to waver, you can put them to rest and into your control once again. If you wish to realize samadhi, if you wish to enter samadhi, put to rest all your wandering thoughts, all the various discords and disorders in your mind. Practice in this way and you will enter into and realize the King of Samadhis Samadhi.*[10]

We now know, without doubt, that sitting crosslegged is in itself the King of Samadhis Samadhi, the entrance into realization. All samadhis are subordinate to this king of samadhis. Crosslegged sitting is the body of suchness, the mind of suchness, the body-mind of suchness, the Buddha-patriarchs in suchness, practice-realization in suchness, the crown of your head in suchness, the direct Dharma lineage in suchness.

Bringing your present human skin, flesh, bone, and marrow together, you form the King of Samadhis Samadhi. The World-Honored One always observed crosslegged sitting. He rightly transmitted it to his disciples as well. He taught it to humans and to devas. It is, in and of itself, the rightly transmitted mind-seal of all the Seven Buddhas.[11]

While Shakyamuni Buddha engaged in crosslegged sitting beneath the Bodhi tree, a period of fifty small kalpas elapsed; sixty regular kalpas passed— an incalculable number of kalpas. But whether he sat crosslegged for twenty-one days or sat for only a short time, he turned the wondrous Dharma Wheel.[12] It is this Dharma to which the Buddha devoted his entire lifetime, teaching and enlightening others—it lacks nothing whatever. Crosslegged sitting is in itself the Buddhist sutra writings. It is at the time of crosslegged sitting that one Buddha encounters another. This is precisely the time when all beings attain to Buddhahood.

After the First Patriarch Bodhidharma came from the west, for a period of nine years he sat crosslegged doing zazen facing a wall at the Shao-lin monastery in Sung-yo.[13] Ever since that time, up until the present day, crowns of heads and clear eyes have been found everywhere throughout China.

---

10. Also from the *Ta chih tu lun*, ch. 7, where it follows immediately after the preceding verse quotation.

11. The (Buddha) mind-seal is what is transmitted in a face-to-face encounter from Buddha to Buddha; here, Dōgen equates it to crosslegged sitting. The *Seven Buddhas* are Shakyamuni and the six Buddhas that appeared in lineal descent prior to him.

12. A kalpa is an inconceivably long period of time. There are different kinds of kalpas and different ways of expressing their lengths. Here the point is that it does not matter whether the Buddha sat for many kalpas or for twenty-one days (as some traditions have it), or for even only a very short time. Crosslegged sitting is beyond all such relativities. At each and every moment, the sitter turns the Dharma Wheel.

13. According to Dōgen, the seated meditation practiced in China prior to the arrival of Bodhidharma was not authentic zazen.

The lifeblood of the First Patriarch's Dharma artery is just crosslegged sitting. Before he arrived in China, crosslegged sitting was totally unknown. After he arrived, it became widely known.

For this reason, when for one lifetime or ten thousand, from beginning to end one does not leave the monastery and engages singlemindedly in crosslegged sitting from morning to night to the exclusion of all else—that is the King of Samadhis Samadhi.

# EIGHT

# Shōji

# 生死

## (Birth and Death)

*Shōji*, the shortest fascicle included in *Shōbōgenzō*, is undated and lacks a colophon. Although not included in Dōgen's own recension of *Shōbōgenzō*, *Shōji* is found in the Sōtō school's official "Honzan" edition. *Shōbōgenzō Shōji* is, with *Shōbōgenzō Zenki*, one of two fascicles that deal specifically with the question of birth-and-death (samsara), the cycle of existence that unenlightened beings repeat endlessly according to their past actions. Samsara is sometimes described as a "sea," limitless and difficult to cross, which Buddhists must negotiate to reach the "other shore" of nirvana. Buddhists vow to save all other beings from the sufferings of birth-and-death. In *SBGZ Shoaku-makusa*, Dōgen wrote that "clarifying birth, clarifying death, is the matter of greatest importance for a Buddhist." However, he rejects an approach that would discard or reject birth-and-death for the bliss of nirvana beyond this world, because birth-and-death is in reality "the life of Buddha," and nirvana is unrealizable apart from samsara. (*Ōkubo*, vol. 1, 778–79).

### SHŌJI

"Since there is a Buddha within birth-and-death, there is no birth-and-death." "Since there is no Buddha within birth-and-death, you are not deluded by birth-and-death." These two utterances were spoken by two Zen masters, Chia-shan and Ting-shan.[1] Being the words of those who have attained the Way, they cannot have been uttered without meaning. Those who would be free from birth-and-death must clearly realize their meaning.

To seek Buddha apart from birth-and-death is like pointing the thills of a cart northward when you want to go south to Yüeh, or facing south to see the northern Dipper; it only furthers the conditions of birth-and-death and deprives you all the more of the Way of deliverance.

Just understand that birth-and-death itself is nirvana, and you will neither hate one as being birth-and-death, nor cherish the other as being nirvana. Only then can you be free of birth-and-death.

It is a mistake to think you pass from life into death. Being one stage of time, life is possessed of before and after. For this reason, the Buddha Dharma teaches that life itself is as such unborn. Being one stage of time as well, cessation of life also is possessed of before and after. Thus it is said that extinction itself is undying. When there is life, there is nothing at all apart from life. When there is death, there is nothing at all apart from death. Therefore, when life comes, you should just give yourself to life; when death comes, you should give yourself to death. You should neither desire them, nor hate them.

Your present birth-and-death itself is the life of Buddha. If you attempt to reject it with aversion, you thereby lose the life of Buddha. If you abide in it, attaching to birth-and-death, you also lose the life of Buddha and are left with only its outward appearance. You attain the mind of Buddha only when there is no hating of birth-and-death and no desiring of nirvana. But do not try to measure it with your mind or explain it with words. When you let go of both

---

1. The full dialogue in which these two quotations appear is found in somewhat different wording in *CTL*, ch. 7. Chia-shan and Ting-shan were walking and talking. Ting-shan said, "No Buddha within birth-and-death is in itself no birth-and-death." Chia-shan said, "Buddha within birth-and-death means no illusion about birth-and-death." They went up the mountain to see master Ta-mei. Chia-shan asked him, "We are unable to decide which of our views is closer to the truth." Ta-mei said, "One is close. One is far." "Which is close?" asked Chia-shan. Ta-mei answered, "You should leave and come again tomorrow." The next day, Chia-shan went once more and put the same question to the master. Ta-mei said, "The one who is close does not ask. The one who asks is not close." (After he had become a temple master himself, Chia-shan said, "At that time I lacked the Dharma eye.")

While both Chia-shan and Ting-shan refer to the oneness of samsara (birth-and-death) and nirvana, the former speaks of liberation from birth-and-death, emphasizing that Buddha is not apart from birth-and-death. The latter indicates the same liberation more clearly, emphasizing that birth-and-death is absolutely birth-and-death, without respect to Buddha or anything else. Although in the full episode quoted above, Ta-mei says that one is close and one far, Dōgen judges them as equal to emphasize the non-duality of samsara and nirvana, and especially to show that not hating samsara and not desiring nirvana is the attainment of Buddhahood. The term "birth-and-death" (*shōji*) is also translated below as "life and death"; the Chinese character for "birth" and "life" are the same.

your body and mind, forget them both, and throw yourself into the house of Buddha, and when functioning begins from the side of Buddha drawing you in to accord with it,[2] then, with no need for any expenditure of either physical or mental effort, you are freed from birth-and-death and become Buddha. Then there can be no obstacle in anyone's mind.

There is an extremely easy way to become Buddha. If you refrain from all evil, do not cling to birth-and-death; work in deep compassion for all sentient beings, respecting those over you and showing compassion for those below you, without any detesting or desiring, worrying or lamentation—that is Buddhahood. Do not search beyond it.

---

2. This sentence is sometimes cited as evidence of Dōgen's affinity with Pure Land thought, and there is a Sōtō tradition that the essay *Shōji* is the record of religious instructions that Dōgen composed for followers of the Pure Land schools. A Pure Land affinity may be admitted if "Buddha," in the expressions "throw yourself into the house of Buddha" and "when functioning begins from the side of Buddha," is taken as a reference to the *tariki* or "other-power" of Amida Buddha. In the overall context of Dōgen's thought, however, it seems more natural to understand "Buddha" in the sense of Buddha-nature or "Original Face," as seen from the side of illusion.

# NINE

# Zazengi
# 坐禅儀

## (The Principles of Zazen)

*Zazengi* was delivered the eleventh month, the first year of Kangen [1243], at Yoshimine-dera, Yoshida, Echizen province. This was the year that Dōgen, then forty-five years old, quit the Kōshō-ji in Uji and went to Echizen province (*Ōkubo*, vol. 1, 88–90).

### ZAZENGI

The practice of Zen (*sanzen*) is zazen.

For zazen, a quiet place is suitable. Lay a cushion of thick matting. Keep the precincts protected, not allowing drafts of air, mist, rain, or dew to enter. In the past, Shakyamuni sat upon a Diamond Seat.[1] Others sat atop large, stable rocks. They all used matting of thick grasses. The place where you sit should be lighted and should not be allowed to grow dark at any time during the day or night. The proper method is to keep it warm in winter and cool in summer.

Involvements of every kind must be cast aside. All worldly affairs must be put to rest. Zazen is not thinking good; it is not thinking bad. It is not

---

1. The Vajra (Diamond) Treasure Seat is where Shakyamuni meditated and attained enlightenment.

mental activity of any kind; it is not contemplation or reflection. Have no intention to become a Buddha. You must cast off your sitting [so that nothing remains].

Be moderate with food and drink, be frugal with your time, and go to zazen as unhesitatingly as you would brush a fire from the top of your head. It was precisely in this way that the Fifth Patriarch of Mount Huang-mei exerted himself single-mindedly in the practice of zazen.[2]

You should wear your surplice when you do zazen. You should use a round cushion filled with rush-grains. The cushion should not be placed so it extends under your legs; it should be no farther forward than a point just beneath the spine, so that your legs cross above the matting and your spine rests above the cushion. This is the method that all Buddhas and all patriarchs use when doing zazen.

You may sit either in the half-lotus or full-lotus posture. In the full-lotus posture, you place your right foot on your left thigh and your left foot on your right thigh. The upper surface of your toes should rest on your thighs. There should be no deviation from this. If you use the half-lotus posture, you simply place your left foot on your right thigh. Your garments should be loosely bound and arranged in an orderly manner. Place your right hand on your left leg and your left hand on your right hand, with your thumb-tips touching. The hands should be placed close to the body in this manner, with the tips of the thumbs joined opposite the navel.

You should sit upright, in correct bodily posture, inclining neither to the left nor to the right, leaning neither forward nor backward. Be sure that your ears are on a plane with your shoulders and that your nose is in line with your navel. Place your tongue against the roof of your mouth and breathe through your nose.[3] Lips and teeth should be closed. Eyes should be open, neither too widely nor too narrowly.[4]

After body and mind are readied in this way, exhale deeply. As you sit, meditating silently and immoveably, think of not thinking. What is thinking of not thinking? Nonthinking. This, in and of itself, is the art of zazen. Zazen is not learning Zen. It is the Dharma Gate of great repose and bliss. It is undefiled practice-realization.

---

2. Hung-jen, the Fifth Chinese Zen patriarch, who succeeded to the Dharma of the Fourth Patriarch Tao-hsin and resided at Mount Huang-mei (Yellow Plum Mountain), in modern Hupeh.

3. Cf. The chief priest [Ju-ching, Dōgen's master] taught Dōgen: "When you do zazen you should rest your tongue on the front upper roof of your mouth. You may also place it against the back of your upper front teeth" (*Hōkyō-ki*, section 41).

4. Eyes are kept open to avoid dozing off. "After forty or fifty years, when zazen has become second nature to you and you never drop you head in a doze, you are not hampered when you do zazen with your eyes shut. Newcomers who are not fully accustomed to sitting, should sit with eyes open" (*Hōkyō-ki*, section 34).

# BIBLIOGRAPHY

*Avatamsaka Sutra* (*Hua-yen ching* 華厳経). T1.9–10

*Bendōwa* 辦道話 (1788 Gentō Sokuchū woodblock edition)

*Ch'an-yüan ch'ing-kuei* 禅苑清規 (*Zen'on shingi*). ZZ.2.16.5

*Cheng-tao ko* 証道歌 (*Shōdō-ka*). T48.2014

*Eihei kōroku* 永平広録: Ōkubo, vol. 2

*Gakudō-yōjinshū* 学道用心集. T82.2581

*Hōkyō-ki* 寶慶記, ed. Ikeda Rosan. Tokyo: Daitō Shuppansha, 1989

*Honzan-ban* 本山版 (edition of *Shōbōgenzō*), compiled 1795–1811

*Hsinhsinming* 信心銘 (*Shinjin-mei*). T48.2060

*Hung-chih sung-ku* 宏智頌古 (*Wanshi juko*). T48

*Ju ta-ch'eng lun* 入大乗論 (*Nyūdaijō-ron*). ZZ.22.4

*Kenzei-ki* 建撕記. *Sōtō-shū zensho*, vol. 17, Tokyo, 1929

*Lin-chi lu* 臨濟録 (*Rinzai-roku*). T47.1985

*Liu-tsu t'an-ching* 六祖壇経 (*Rokusodan-gyō*). T48.2008

*Lotus Sutra* 法華経 (*Hokke-kyō*). T9.262

*Mo-ho chih-kuan* 摩訶止観 (*Maka-shikan*). T46.1911

*Nirvana Sutra* 涅槃経 (*Nehan-gyō*). T12

*Pi-yen lu* 碧巌録 (*Hekigan-roku*). T48.2003

*P'u-sa ying-lo ching* 菩薩瓔珞経 (*Bosatsu yōraku-kyō*). T24.1010–23

*Pu-teng lu* 普燈録 (*Futō-roku*). ZZ2.2.10

*The Record of Lin-chi*, trans. Ruth Sasaki. Kyoto: Institute for Zen Studies, 1975

*She ta-ch'eng-lun* 摂大乗論 (*Shō daijō-ron*). T31

*Shōbōgenzō chūkai zensho* 正法眼蔵註解全書, 11 vols. Tokyo, 1956–1957

*Shōbōgenzō keiteki* 正法眼蔵啓迪, 3 vols. Daihōrin, Tokyo, 1940

*Shōbōgenzō zuimonki* 正法眼蔵随聞記: Ōkubo, vol. 2

*Ssu-shih-erh chang ching* 四十二章経 (*Shijūnishō-gyō*). T17.784

*Ta-ch'eng ch'i-hsin lun* 大乗起信論 (*Daijō kishin-ron*). T32.1666

*Ta-chih tu lun* 大智度論 (*Mahā prajñā-pāramitā shastra*).T25

*T'ien-sheng kuang-teng lu* 天聖広灯録 (*Tenshō kōtō-roku*). ZZ.2b8.4–5

*Tsa-pao-tsang ching* 雑宝蔵経 (*Zōhōzō-kyō*). T203

*Tso-an ko* 草庵歌 (*Sōan-ka*). T51.461

*Ts'ung-jung lu* 従容録 (*Shōyō-roku*). T48.226–292

*Tung-shan lu* 洞山録 (*Tōzan-roku*). T47.1986

*Vimalakirti Sutra* 維摩経 (*Wei-mo ching*). T14.475

*Wu-men kuan* 無門関 (*Mumonkan*). T48.2006

*Wu-teng hui-yüan* 五燈会元 (*Gotō-egen*). ZZ2b.10.5

# INDEX